IN THE THE BEGINNING...

IN THE BEGINNING...

ISAAC ASIMOV

A Stonesong Press Book

CROWN PUBLISHERS, INC.
New York

Inquiries should be addressed to Crown Publishers, Inc., One Park Avenue, New York, New York 10016

Printed in the United States of America

Published simultaneously in Canada by General Publishing Company Limited

Library of Congress Cataloging in Publication Data

Asimov, Isaac, 1920–
    In the beginning.

    1. Bible and science. 2. Bible. O.T. Genesis
I-XI—Criticism, interpretation, etc. I. Title
BS651.A75 1981   213   80-24754
ISBN: 0-517-543362

10 9 8 7 6 5 4 3 2 1

First Edition

Dedicated to:

Izzy and Annie Adler,
who have advanced degrees in lovability.

Introduction

The Bible is the most-read book that has ever existed, and there are uncounted millions of people in the world who, even today, take it for granted that it is the inspired word of God; that it is literally true at every point; that there are no mistakes or contradictions except where these can be traced to errors in copying or in translation.

There are undoubtedly many who do not realize that the Authorized Version (the "King James Bible"), the one with which English-speaking Protestants are most familiar, is, in fact, a translation, and who therefore believe that every one of *its* words is inspired and infallible.

Against these strong, unwavering, and undeviating beliefs, the slowly developing views of scientists have always had to fight.

Biological evolution, for instance, is considered a fact of nature by almost all biologists. There may be and, indeed, are many arguments over the details of the mechanics of evolution, but none over the fact—just as we may not completely understand the workings of an automobile engine and yet be certain that a car in good working order will move if we turn the key and step on the gas.

There are millions of people, however, who are strongly and emotionally opposed to the notion of biological evolution, even though they know little or nothing about the evidence and rationale behind it. It is enough for them that the Bible states thus-and-so. The argument ends there.

Well, then, what does the Bible say, and what does science say? Where, if anywhere, do they agree? Where do they disagree?

That is what this book is about.

It does not argue one way or the other. It offers no

1

polemics. It merely considers the verses of the Bible, line by line and, indeed, word by word, discusses the content and meaning, and compares them with the scientific view that pertains to the passage.

Nor does it do this for the entire Bible, for the chief area of dispute lies in the very beginning of the Bible— the first eleven chapters of the Book of Genesis.

The Bible, as a whole, deals with the legendary Abram (called Abraham later in life) and his descendants, but in the first eleven chapters of the Book of Genesis, there is a quick overview of earlier events from the creation of the Universe to the birth of Abram about 2000 B.C.

This period of primeval history is based on two documents, according to those who have most carefully studied the Bible: the J-document and the P-document.

The J-document, which is the older, contains dramatic early legends that were current among the people of Israel and Judah. The tales of the J-document may have been written down and reached their present form some time before 700 B.C., when Assyria from its base in the Tigris-Euphrates valley (modern Iraq) was the strongest kingdom in western Asia.

Even before Assyria became powerful, the culture of the Tigris-Euphrates dominated western Asia, even as far back as 3400 B.C., when the Sumerians (who lived there then) invented writing. The Sumerian legends and their theories of the creation of the Universe and of early history spread to all the surrounding peoples and exerted a strong influence on them (just as Western theories of the creation of the Universe and of early history have spread to and influenced surrounding non-Western peoples today).

The P-document is later and was gathered and put together during the time when the people of Judah (the Jews) were in captivity in the Tigris-Euphrates region in the sixth century B.C. At that time, the dominant tribe of the region was the Chaldeans, and their capital was in Babylon, so that the P-document picked up what we might call Chaldean or Babylonian views of cosmic history—which in turn were based on nearly three thousand years of thought dating back to the Sumerians.

The two documents were combined by reverent editors, concerned to do as little damage to either as possible. The first eleven chapters of the Book of Genesis reached their present shape by the time the Jews returned to Jerusalem from Babylonian exile—say, 500 B.C.

All through the first eleven chapters of the Book of Genesis, there is a strong tinge of the Tigris-Euphrates; a Sumerian/Assyrian/Babylonian thread that is unmistakable.

This is not necessarily bad. The people of the Tigris-Euphrates region were the most sophisticated people in the world at the time and had elaborated the closest approach to what we might call science. They were ahead of other civilizations in this respect—the Egyptian, the Indian, the Chinese, the Cretan—from the time when writing was invented to the time when the Bible took on its present shape, a period of three thousand years.

What's more, the Biblical writers and editors were thoughtful men who borrowed selectively, choosing what they considered good and rejecting what seemed nonsensical or unedifying. They labored to produce something that was as reasonable and as useful as possible.

In doing so, they succeeded wonderfully. There is no version of primeval history, preceding the discoveries of modern science, that is as rational and as inspiring as that of the first eleven chapters of the Book of Genesis.

Nevertheless, humanity does progress. Succeeding generations learn more and deduce more. If the primeval history of the Book of Genesis falls short of what science now believes to be the truth, the fault cannot lie with the Biblical writers, who did the best they could with the material available to them. If they had written those early chapters of Genesis knowing what we know today, we can be certain they would have written it completely differently.

And having said all that, we will now turn to the Book of Genesis and begin our task.

The First Book of Moses,[1] Called

GENESIS [2]

Chapter 1 [3]

1. By ancient tradition, the first five books of the Bible were written by Moses, the folk hero who, according to the account given in the second through fifth books of the Bible, rescued the Israelites from Egyptian slavery.

Modern scholars are convinced that this theory of authorship is not tenable and that the early books of the Bible are not the single work of any man, and certainly not of Moses. Rather, they are a carefully edited compilation of material from a number of sources.

The theory of multiple authorship of the Bible dates only from the nineteenth century, however.

In 1611, when King James I of England appointed fifty-four scholars to produce an English translation of the Bible suitable for English-speaking Protestants, no one questioned the tradition of the Mosaic authorship of the five books. The Bible produced by these scholars is the "Authorized Version" (authorized by the king, that is, in his capacity as head of the Anglican Church). The Authorized Version is commonly referred to as the King James Bible. It is the one I am using in this book because, even today, it is *the* Bible in the minds of almost all English-speaking people. There have been better translations since, to be sure, but none can match the King James Version for sheer poetry.

In the King James, the initial book of the Bible is referred to as "The First Book of Moses."

2. The First Book of Moses begins, in the original Hebrew, with the word *bereshith*. It was not uncommon in Biblical times to refer to a book by its first word or words. (Papal bulls, to this day, are named for the two Latin words with which they begin.)

The Hebrew name for the First Book of Moses is therefore *Bereshith*. Since the word happens to mean "in the

5

beginning," and since the First Book of Moses starts its tale with the creation of the Universe, it is an apt name. (In fact, I use the phrase as the title for the book you are holding.)

The Bible was first translated into another language, Greek, in the third century B.C. In the Greek version of the Bible, the Hebrew habit of using the first words as the name was not followed, and descriptive names were used instead. The First Book of Moses was named *Genesis,* a Greek word meaning "coming into being." This is also an apt name, and the Greek *Genesis* is commonly used as the title of the first Book of the Bible, even in English translation.

3. Early manuscripts of the Bible did not divide the various books into chapters and verses. It was only little by little that such divisions appeared. The present system of chapters and verses first appeared in an English Bible in 1560.

The divisions are not always logical, but there is no way of abandoning them or changing them, for they have been used in reference, in commentaries, and in concordances for four centuries now, and one cannot wipe out the usefulness of all these books.

---

1 *In the beginning* [4] *God* [5] *created* [6] *the heaven* [7] *and the earth.* [8]

---

4. The very first phrase in the Bible states that there was a beginning to things.

Why not? It seems natural. Those objects with which we are familiar have a beginning. You and I were born, and before that we did not exist, at least not in our present form. The same is true of other human beings, of plants and animals and, in fact, of all living things, as far as we know from common observation.

We are surrounded, moreover, by all the works of humanity, and all these were, in one way or another, fashioned by human beings; before that, they did not exist, at least in their fashioned form.

It seems natural to feel that if all things alive and human-fashioned had a beginning, then the rule might be universal, and that things that are neither alive nor human-fashioned might also have had a beginning.

At any rate, primitive attempts to explain the Universe start with an explanation of its beginning. This seems so natural a thing that it is doubtful if anyone ever questioned the concept of a beginning in early times, however much disagreement there may have been over the details.

And in the scientific view, there is also considered to be a beginning, not only for Earth, but for the entire Universe.

Since the Bible and science both state that heaven and earth had a beginning, does this represent a point of agreement between them?

Yes, of course—but it is a trivial agreement. There is an enormous difference between the Biblical statement of beginning and the scientific statement of beginning, which I will explain because it illuminates all subsequent agreements between the Biblical and scientific point of view; and, for that matter, all subsequent disagreements.

Biblical statements rest on authority. If they are accepted as the inspired word of God, all argument ends there. There is no room for disagreement. The statement is final and absolute for all time.

A scientist, on the other hand, is committed to accepting nothing that is not backed by acceptable evidence. Even if the matter in question seems obviously certain on the face of it, it is all the better if it is backed by such evidence.

Acceptable evidence is that which can be observed and measured in such a way that subjective opinion is minimized. In other words, different people repeating the observations and measurements with different instruments at different times and in different places should come to the same conclusion. Furthermore, the deductions made from the observations and measurements must follow certain accepted rules of logic and reason.

Such evidence is "scientific evidence," and ideally, scientific evidence is "compelling." That is, people who study the observations and measurements, and the deductions made therefrom, feel compelled to agree with the conclusions even if, in the beginning, they felt strong doubts in the matter.

One may argue, of course, that scientific reasoning is not the only path to truth; that there are inner revelations, or intuitive grasps, or blinding insights, or overwhelming authority that all reach the truth more firmly and more surely than scientific evidence does.

That may be so, but none of these alternate paths to truth is compelling. Whatever one's internal certainty, it remains difficult to transfer that certainty simply by saying, "But I'm sure of it." Other people very often remain unsure and skeptical.

Whatever the authority of the Bible, there has never been a time in history when more than a minority of the human species has accepted that authority. And even among those who accepted the authority, differences in interpretation have been many and violent, and on every possible point, no one interpretation has ever won out over all others.

So intense have been the differences and so unable has any one group been to impress other groups with its version of the "truth" that force has very often been resorted to. There is no need here to go into the history of Europe's wars of religion or of the burning of heretics, to give examples.

Science, too, has seen its share of arguments, disputes, and polemics; scientists are human, and scientific ideals (like all other ideals) are rarely approached in practice. An extraordinary number of such arguments, disputes, and polemics have been settled on one side or the other, and the general scientific opinion has then swung to that side because of *compelling* evidence.

And yet, no matter how compelling the evidence, it remains true, in science, that more and better evidence may turn up, that hidden errors and false assumptions may be uncovered, that an unexpected incompleteness may make itself visible, and that yesterday's "firm" conclusion may suddenly twist and change into a deeper and better conclusion.

It follows, then, that the Biblical statement that earth

and heaven had a beginning is authoritative and absolute, but not compelling; while the scientific statement that earth and heaven had a beginning is compelling, but not authoritative and absolute. There is a disagreement there that is deeper and more important than the superficial agreement of the words themselves.

And even the superficial agreement of the words themselves disappears as soon as we ask a further question.

For instance, if we grant the existence of a beginning, suppose we ask just *when* that beginning took place.

The Bible does not tell us when, directly. Indeed, the Bible does not date a single event in any of the books of the King James Version in any way that would help us tie those events into a specific time in the system of chronology we use.

Nevertheless, the question of when the Creation took place has aroused curiosity, and various Biblical scholars have made every effort to deduce its date by using various statements found in the Bible as indirect evidence.

They did not come to precisely the same answer. The generally accepted conclusion among Jewish scholars, for instance, was that the date of the Creation was October 7, 3761 B.C.

James Ussher, the Anglican archbishop of Armagh, Ireland, decided in 1654, on the other hand, that the Creation took place at 9 A.M. on October 23, 4004 B.C. (Ussher's calculations for this and for the dating of other events in the Bible are usually found in all the page headings of the King James Bible.) Other calculations put the Creation as far back as 5509 B.C.

Thus, the usual estimates for the age of the heaven and earth from Biblical data run from about fifty-seven hundred to seventy-five hundred years. It is over this point that the Biblical conclusions represent an enormous disagreement with the conclusions of science.

The weight of scientific evidence is that Earth, and the solar system generally, came into being in approximately their present form about 4.6 billion years ago. The Universe, generally, came into being, it would seem, about fifteen billion years ago.

The age of Earth, then, according to science, is about

9

six hundred thousand times the age according to the Bible, and the age of the Universe, according to science, is at least two million times the age according to the Bible.

In the light of that discrepancy, the mere agreement between the Bible and science that there was, in fact, a beginning, loses most of its value.

5. God is introduced at once as the motive force behind the Universe. His existence is taken for granted in the Bible, and one might, indeed, argue that the existence of God is self-evident.

Consider: All living things are born through the activities of previous living things. If there were, indeed, a beginning, as the Bible and science both agree, how then did the first living things come into existence?

If there were indeed a beginning, how did all the natural objects—land and sea, hills and valleys, sky and earth—come into being? All artificial objects were fashioned by human beings; who or what then fashioned natural objects?

The usual manner in which this is presented is something like, "A watch implies a watchmaker." Since it is inconceivable that an object as intricate as a watch came into being spontaneously, it must therefore have been fashioned; how much more must something as intricate as the Universe have been fashioned!

In early times, the analogy was drawn much more tightly. Since human beings can, by blowing, create a tiny wind rushing out of their nostrils and mouths, the wind in nature must, by analogy, be the product of a much more powerful being blowing through nostrils and mouth. If a horse-and-chariot is a common way of progressing over land, then a glowing horse-and-chariot must be the means by which the sun is carried over the sky.

In the myths, every natural phenomenon is likely to have a humanlike creature performing functions analogous to those of the human actions we know, so that *nothing* in nature takes place spontaneously.

These myriad specialized divinities were often pictured as at odds with each other and as producing a disorderly Universe. As thought grew deeper, the tendency was to suppose one divine being who is responsible for everything, who directs humanity, Earth, and the whole Universe, combining it all into a harmonious whole directed toward some specific end.

It is this sophisticated picture of a monotheistic God that the Bible presents—but one who constantly engages himself in the minutiae of his creation. Even under a monotheistic religion, popular thought imagines myriad angels and saints taking on specialized functions so that a form of polytheism (under a supreme monarch) exists.

In the last four centuries, however, scientists have built up an alternate picture of the Universe. The sun doesn't move across the sky; its apparent motion is due to Earth's rotation. The wind doesn't have to be produced by giant lungs; its existence arises through the spontaneous action of air subjected to uneven heating by the sun. In other words, a moving sun does not imply a horse-and-chariot, after all; nor does the wind imply the mouth of a blower.

The natural phenomena of Earth and of the Universe have seemed to fall into place bit by bit as behavior that is random, spontaneous, unwilled, and that takes place within the constraints of the "laws of nature."

Scientists grew increasingly reluctant to suppose that the workings of the laws of nature were ever interfered with (something that would be defined as a "miracle"). Certainly, no such interference was ever observed, and the tales of such interferences in the past came to seem increasingly dubious.

In short, the scientific view sees the Universe as following its own rules blindly, without either interference or direction.

That still leaves it possible that God created the Universe to begin with and designed the laws of nature that govern its behavior. From this standpoint, the Universe might be viewed as a wind-up toy, which God has wound up once and for all and which is now winding down and working itself out in all its intricacy without having to be touched at all.

If so, that reduces God's involvement to a minimum and makes one wonder if he is needed at all.

So far, scientists have not uncovered any evidence that

would hint that the workings of the Universe require the action of a divine being. On the other hand, scientists have uncovered no evidence that indicates that a divine being does *not* exist.

If scientists have not proven either that God exists or that he does not exist, then, from the scientific viewpoint, are we entitled to believe either alternative?

Not really. It is not reasonable to demand proof of a negative and to accept the positive in the absence of such a proof. After all, if science has not succeeded in proving that God does not exist, neither has it succeeded in proving that Zeus does not exist, or Marduk, or Thoth, or any of the myriads of gods postulated by all sorts of myth-makers. If the failure of proof of nonexistence is taken as proof of existence, then we must conclude that *all* exist.

Yet that leaves us with the final, nagging question: "But where did all this come from? How did the Universe come into being in the first place?"

If one tries to answer, "The Universe was always there; it is eternal," then one comes up against the uncomfortable concept of eternity and the irresistible assumption that everything had to have a beginning.

Out of sheer exhaustion one longs to solve everything by saying, "God made the Universe!" That gives us a start, at least.

But then we find that we have escaped eternity only by postulating it, for we are not even allowed to ask the question, "Who made God?" The question itself is blasphemous. God is eternal, by definition.

If, then, we are going to be stuck with eternity in any case, there seems some advantage to a science that lives by observing and measuring, to choose an eternal something that can at least be observed and measured—the Universe itself, rather than God.

The notion of an eternal Universe introduces a great many difficulties, some of them apparently (at least in the present state of our scientific knowledge) insuperable, but scientists are not disturbed by difficulties—those make up the game. If all the difficulties were gone and all the questions answered, the game of science would be over. (Scientists suspect that will never happen.)

There, then, is perhaps the most fundamental disagreement between the Bible and science. The Bible describes a Universe created by God, maintained by him, and intimately and constantly directed by him, while science describes a Universe in which it is not necessary to postulate the existence of God at all.

This is *not* to say, by the way, that scientists are all atheists or that any of them must be atheists of necessity. There are many scientists who are as firmly religious as any nonscientist. Nevertheless, such scientists, if they are competent professionals, must operate on two levels. Whatever their faith in God in ordinary life, they must leave God out of account while engaged in their scientific observations. They can never explain a particular puzzling phenomenon by claiming it to be the result of God's suspension of natural law.

6. The first act of God recorded in the Bible is that of the creation of the Universe. But since God is eternal, there must have been an infinitely long period of time before he set our Universe into motion. What was he doing during that infinitely long period of time?

When St. Augustine was asked that question, he is supposed to have roared, "Creating Hell for those who ask questions like that!"

Ignoring St. Augustine (if we dare), we might speculate. God might, for instance, have spent the time creating an endless hierarchy of angels. For that matter, he might have created an endless number of universes, one after the other, each for its own purpose, with our own being merely the current member of the series, to be followed by an equally endless number of successors. Or God might, until the moment of the Creation, have done nothing but commune with his infinite self.

All possible answers to the question are merely suppositions, however, since there is no evidence for any one of them. There is not only no scientific evidence for them; there is not even any Biblical evidence. The answers belong entirely to the world of legend.

But then if we switch to the world of science and think of an eternal Universe, we must ask what the Universe was like before it took on its present form about fifteen billion years ago. There are some speculations. The Universe may have existed through eternity as an infinitely thin scattering of matter and energy that very slowly coalesced into a tiny dense object, the "cosmic egg," which exploded to form the Universe we now have, a Universe that will expand forever until it is an infinitely thin scattering of matter and energy again.

Or else there is an alternation of expansion and contraction, an endless series of cosmic eggs, each of which explodes to form a Universe. Our own present Universe is only the current member of an endless series.

Science, however, has found no way as yet of penetrating into a time earlier than that of the cosmic egg that exploded to form our Universe. The Bible and science agree in being unable to say anything certainly about what happened before the beginning.

There is this difference. The Bible will never be able to tell us. It has reached its final form, and it simply doesn't say. Science, on the other hand, is still developing, and the time may come when it can answer questions that, at present, it cannot.

7. By heaven, in this verse, is meant the vault of the sky and the permanent objects within it—the sun, moon, planets, and stars. The Bible views this vault as the Babylonians did (and the Egyptians, the Greeks, and all the early peoples, apparently without exception); that is, as a solid, semicircular dome overspreading Earth. This is the Biblical view throughout. Thus, in Revelation, the last book of the Bible, the final end of the heaven is described thus: "The heaven departed as a scroll when it is rolled together" (Revelation 6:14). This quoted a passage in the Old Testament (Isaiah 34:4) and clearly shows the heaven to have been viewed as no thicker, in proportion to its extent, than a sheet of parchment.

In the scientific view, however, the sky is not a simple vault, but is a vast outstretching of space-time into which our telescopes have probed for distances of ten billion light-years, where each light-year is 5.88 trillion miles long.

8. The "heaven and the earth" form a definite geometrical shape in the Bible. The earth is a flat, probably circular, area of extent large enough to hold those kingdoms known to the Biblical writers. The heaven is a semispherical vault that nestles down over the earth. Human beings, by this picture, seem to live on the floor of a world that is inside a hollow semisphere.

It is so described in the Book of Isaiah: "It is he [God] that sitteth upon the circle of the earth . . . that stretched out the heavens as a curtain, and spreadeth them out as a tent to dwell in" (Isaiah 40:22).

The vault of heaven would require support to keep it from collapsing, if we judge from earthly structures. The support might be a supernatural being (like the Greek myth of Atlas) or something more mechanical. The Bible has a passage that reads, "The pillars of heaven tremble" (Job 26:11).

All this is utterly different from the scientific view of Earth as a sphere, suspended in emptiness, that rotates on its axis, revolves about the sun, takes part in the sun's revolution about the center of the Galaxy, and is surrounded by a largely empty and virtually illimitable Universe.

---

2 *And the earth was without form and void;[9] and darkness [10] was [11] upon the face of the deep.[12] And the Spirit of God [13] moved upon the face of the waters.*

---

9. A question arises here. Did God create Earth "without form and void" (the two terms emphasize each other, for Earth is not only "without form," but it is also "void"—that is, "empty" of form)?

Or was Earth "without form and void" to begin with, and did the process of creation begin from there?

Everything depends on how the first verse in the Bible is interpreted. One might assume that the first verse is a simple declarative statement. "In the beginning God created the heaven and the earth"—and there it all was "without form and void," created so out of nothing.

Or we might assume that the first verse is a mere introductory summary, almost a chapter heading—The Creation of the Heaven and the Earth. Then there follows the actual description of how it was done.

Modern scholars seem to think the second interpretation is the more likely. The Anchor Bible, published in 1964, begins Genesis thus: "When God set about to create heaven and earth—the world being then a formless waste . . ."

This would make it seem that the raw material of the world was there all along and that God's role in the Creation was that of shaping the raw material of the Universe into the finished form, much as a potter shapes the raw clay into a vessel. In fact, the metaphor is used in the Bible: "But now, O Lord, thou art our father; we are the clay, and thou our potter; and we all are the work of thy hand" (Isaiah 64:8).

This was the Greek view, too, for in their mythology, there was "Chaos" (meaning "disorder") in the beginning of things. All the material out of which the world was formed was randomly mixed, and creation consisted in imposing order ("Cosmos") upon it.

This is not too far different from some aspects of the scientific view of Creation. If we confined ourselves to the solar system, the present view of scientists is that it was formed from a vast cloud of dust and gas. It is easy to see that the original cloud of dust and gas represents matter in complete disorder and is an approach to chaos.

As the cloud slowly swirled, its own gravitational field drew it together, causing it to whirl faster and faster in accordance with the law of conservation of angular momentum. Most of the matter finds its way into the central core, becoming the sun, but turbulence produces secondary, much smaller concentrations that make up the planets, including Earth. Tertiary, still smaller concentrations form the satellites.

Certainly, we see here Cosmos arising out of Chaos, order out of disorder.

The solar system is not, however, all there is to the

Universe. Our sun, with its attendant planets, is only one such object out of a few hundred billion which, taken together, form a flattened, whirling disk of stars, called the Galaxy.

Scientists think that the entire Galaxy (and each of a hundred billion or so other galaxies) was formed out of a whirling cloud of dust and gas a hundred billion times as massive as the one out of which our single solar system was formed. There again it would seem that order is formed out of disorder, as a mass of swirling gas and dust "without form and void" breaks up into billions upon billions of individual stars (many or most of them with planetary systems, presumably, though for this we do not yet have direct evidence).

In one respect there is a great difference between the Biblical view at this point and the scientific view. The Biblical view would make it appear that Earth and the rest of the Universe were all created at the same time.

In the scientific view, Earth and the entire solar system are latecomers in the Universe. When the solar system formed out of its dust cloud, the Galaxy had already existed in much its present shape for some ten billion years.

The sun is, in fact, a "second-generation star" formed out of a cloud of dust and gas that contained within it the remains of earlier stars that had lived out their lifetimes and exploded, strewing their material into space.

If we leave that discrepancy out of consideration, there remain two points to be made out of this "Chaos-into-Cosmos" progression, which the Biblical tale of creation and the scientific view have in common.

First, it implies the eternal existence of the raw material out of which the Universe is fashioned, so that the problem of "But where did it all come from?" is no more answered by the Bible than by science.

Second, there is an important scientific generalization, the second law of thermodynamics, which holds that, on the whole, there is a general, overall progression from order to disorder. The formation of the solar system and of the galaxies would seem to move in a direction counter to that which the second law of thermodynamics would enforce.

Does this imply that the laws of science are inadequate to explain the creation of the solar system and the galaxies and that we must postulate the existence of God—who alone is capable of overriding the second law of thermodynamics when necessary? This is something I will return to.

10. The verse goes on to emphasize the chaos in the beginning, for darkness is a symbol of chaos.

That is natural. An orderly nature with everything in its place is clearly evident in the light. Let the darkness fall, particularly in a strange place, and we no longer have the benefit of order. We do not know where anything is, and we must stumble and grope as though chaos had come again.

This, too, fits the scientific view, in a way, for the original cloud of dust and gas out of which the solar system was formed (or the larger clouds out of which the galaxies were formed) was dark.

11. The word "was" is printed in italics in the King James Version. This does not have the usual indication of emphasis that italics often do.

In endeavoring to translate each Hebrew word of the original Bible into English, there are occasions when additional English words had to be added to make sense. Thus the Hebrew words, literally translated, would be "and darkness upon the face of the deep." In English "was" has to be added, and it is italicized to indicate that it does not stand for any word in the original.

Later English translations of the Bible did not display the exaggerated respect for the literal Hebrew words and showed no embarrassment at having to add words to make English sense. In this book, therefore, the italicizations of the King James Version will be ignored.

12. Another symbol of Chaos is "the deep"; that is, the ocean. Compared to the dry land surface upon which human beings live, the ocean is a random tumble of matter, always moving and heaving and, in the course of a storm, raging with a power incomparably greater than anything human beings could control.

The picture of the Universe at its beginning is as of something that is as chaotic as the sea, a concept the Biblical writers obtained from the Babylonians.

The first chapter of Genesis is taken from the P-document and did not appear in its present form until after the Babylonian captivity. It seems to have been adapted by the priestly leaders of the Jews (the "P" of "P-document" stands for "priest") from the Babylonian myth of creation, which was itself a modification of an earlier Sumerian one.

In the Babylonian myth, the forces of Chaos were represented by Tiamat, as wild, as lawless, as powerful as the sea. The gods who represent the forces of order quail before her, but finally Marduk, the chief god of the Babylonian pantheon, dares to oppose her. Marduk overcomes and slays Tiamat in a vast, cosmic struggle. Then, out of the remains of Tiamat, Marduk fashioned the orderly Universe.

"The deep" is the English translation of the Hebrew word *tehom*, and it is possible that this is related to the word "Tiamat." God, however, is not pictured here as engaged in single combat with the "deep," wresting order from it by force of arms. The writers of the P-document were too sophisticated for that. In their view, God was the ruler of the Universe, and his word and will were sufficient. There was nothing, not even Chaos, that could do anything but obey.

Nevertheless, there are verses elsewhere in the Bible that seem to hark back to an older view of single combat between the God of order and the dragon of Chaos, out of which combat the Universe was created. Thus, we have:

"Thou didst divide the sea by thy strength: thou brakest the heads of the dragons in the waters. Thou brakest the heads of Leviathan in pieces..." (Psalm 74:13-14)

"Awake, awake, put on strength, O arm of the Lord; awake, as in the ancient days, in the generations of old. Art thou not it that hath cut Rahab and wounded the dragon?" (Isaiah 51:9)

19

It is likely, of course, that the references here are to Egypt and to the parting of the Red Sea, but even if that is so, the choice of words makes it sound like a physical combat with a dragon, and that is an irresistible reminder of the Babylonian tale of Marduk and Tiamat.

If we seek for the dragon of Chaos in the scientific view of the origin of the Universe, we might find an analogy in the waste of swirling dust and gas out of which the solar system formed, or the far larger one out of which the Galaxy formed. Those whirls of dust and gas were an even better representation of Chaos, perhaps, than is the sea.

13. The word "spirit" is the translation of the Hebrew word *ruakh,* which means "breath." It seems a great stretch from the prosaic "breath" to the mysterious and transcendent "spirit," but it seems so only because we have invested "spirit" with mystery and transcendence it perhaps doesn't deserve. It is from the Latin *spiritus,* which means "a breath," and we find it as such in the English "respiration."

The phrase "Spirit of God" is therefore "the breath of God." God is viewed by the writers of the P-document as the most immaterial thing with which they are acquainted—invisible, impalpable air. (In the scientific view, air is as material as water, soil, or metal.) The breath of God—and wind—blew over the waters, and that is all that is left, in this account, of the cosmic battle between the principles of Order and Chaos.

---

3 *And God said,*[14] *Let there be light:* [15] *and there was light.*[16]

---

14. God speaks for the first time. Having begun with Chaos, he now begins to impose Order.

15. If we were writing the Bible today, we would enclose God's first remark in quotation marks, thus, "Let there be light," and this is indeed done in contemporary

translations such as the Revised Standard Version. At the time the King James Version was prepared, however, quotation marks had not yet come into use, and they have been omitted from all later editions of that version.

Nor can I bring myself to insert quotation marks with the same careless shrug with which I omit the italicizations. Quotation marks would somehow alter the flavor of a book which (together with Shakespeare) represents the supreme achievement of the English language, and this I am not willing to do.

This command, by the way, represents a significant departure from the Babylonian myth of Creation. In the Babylonian myth, Tiamat lies enveloped in darkness, and from the gods, who approach her and must somehow overcome her, there emanates light. Light is an attribute of the gods.

The writers of the P-document, however, will have no aspect of Order coexistent with God—not even light, the quintessential symbol of Order as darkness is the symbol of Chaos. Even light must be created or it cannot exist, and God creates it.

16. There are two places in the scientific view of the beginning of things as they now are where the command "Let there be light" might seem to have an application.

First, consider the formless, chaotic mass of dust and gas slowly collapsing on the way to the formation of the solar system. As the mass collapses inward, its energy of motion is converted into heat, and the center of the whole, where the gathering matter is densest, grows hotter and hotter. The temperature rises into the thousands of degrees and, eventually, into the millions of degrees.

As the heat at the center rises, the atoms of which the matter is composed move more and more quickly and smash into each other in random collisions with greater and greater force. The outer shells of electrons boil off and are smashed off. The bare nuclei at the centers of the atoms smash into each other without being impeded by intervening electrons and fuse with each other into more complex nuclei. This "nuclear fusion" produces a great deal of energy that is, in part, converted into electromagnetic radiation that streams out from the central regions of the cloud, which has now condensed into the sun. The electromagnetic radiation streaming out from the sun in all directions, we can detect, in part, as light.

In short, as the cloud condenses to form the sun, there comes a point when the sun ignites with a central nuclear fire and begins to shine. At that point, the sun "turns on," perhaps quite rapidly, and it is as though there were the command of "Let there be light."

Secondly, there is an earlier and an even more dramatic point at which we might view the command as having been given.

The solar system was formed nearly five billion years ago and the Galaxy, of which it forms part, billions of years before that. The Galaxy, however, is only one vast conglomeration of stars among many others like itself. There may be, in the Universe, as many as a hundred billion different galaxies, each containing many billions (or, in some cases, trillions) of stars.

In the 1920s, it was discovered that these galaxies exist in clusters that are receding from each other. It was found to be consistent with Einstein's General Theory of Relativity (advanced in 1916) that the Universe was steadily expanding.

This means that, in the future, the Universe will be larger than it is now and that the matter within it will be spread out more thinly. It also means that, in the past, the Universe was smaller than it is now and that the matter within it was less spread out.

In fact, if we look far enough back in time, we can imagine a period when all the matter in the Universe was clumped together into a single body. The first to propose this was the Belgian astronomer (and Catholic priest) Georges Lemaître in 1927. Calling the single body that existed at the beginning "the cosmic egg," he suggested that its explosion led to the formation of the Universe as we now know it and that the galactic clusters recede from each other as part of the effect of that long-ago explosion.

Since Lemaître's time, astronomers have done their

best to figure out what the cosmic egg was like and what the stages of its explosion were like.

If we imagine the Universe running backward in time, then we see all the galaxies coming together, and the effect is just that of the matter in a cloud of dust and gas coming together. The center grows hot.

Just as the sun grew hot as it formed forward in time, so the cosmic egg must grow hot as it forms backward in time. The heat of the sun, which resulted from the contraction of just one star's worth of matter, is nothing at all compared to the heat of the cosmic egg formed from the contraction of the matter making up a billion trillion stars.

The cosmic egg was therefore inconceivably hot.

Suppose we begin with this super-hot cosmic egg and imagine time flowing forward again. The cosmic egg explodes in the largest conceivable explosion (the "big bang"), and its fragments are at first entirely too hot for matter, as we know it, to exist. Initially, the products formed in the explosion are energy. In tiny fractions of a second, the temperature dropped precipitously, and the Universe became cool enough to form certain fundamental particles of matter. Today, however, the Universe is *too cool* to allow these particles to exist.

A full second after the big bang, the temperature of the Universe had dropped to ten billion degrees, about what it is at the center of the largest stars, and the ordinary subatomic particles we know today came into existence. Later, ordinary atoms formed.

It was, however, not until about a million years after the big bang, by which time the temperature of the Universe had dropped to five thousand degrees (that of the surface of the sun), that matter came to predominate in the Universe. Until then, it was energy that predominated.

(By now, fifteen billion years later, the temperature of the Universe has dropped to an average of three degrees above absolute zero, though, obviously, there remain hot spots.)

It is rather dramatic to imagine that "Let there be

light" marked the big bang and the initial period of energy-dominance. Light, after all, is a form of energy.

In fact, we might paraphrase the first three verses of Genesis as follows to make them fit the scientific view of the beginning of the Universe:

"To begin with, fifteen billion years ago, the Universe consisted of a structureless cosmic egg which exploded in a vast outpouring of energy."

There are some points that must be made, though. The cosmic egg may be structureless (as far as we know), but it apparently represented a very orderly conglomeration of matter. Its explosion represented a vast shift in the direction of disorder, and ever since, the amount of disorder in the Universe has been increasing. (Scientists have invented the term "entropy," which, among other things, is a measure of the amount of disorder in a system.)

Within the vast shift toward disorder involved in the big bang and the expansion of the Universe, it is possible for there to be local shifts in the direction of order, so that the galaxies can form and within them individual stars, including our sun. Earth can form along with the sun, and on Earth there can be a growth of complexity and order to form life and for that life to evolve.

Nevertheless, *on the whole,* the Universe moves, with time, from order to disorder, from low entropy to high entropy. It is possible that in the final end of the Universe, the situation will be one of maximum entropy, or complete chaos. In short, the Universe is moving from Cosmos to Chaos, from Order to Disorder, in the reverse direction of that imagined by the various mythological accounts of the Creation—including the Biblical account.

The existence of the cosmic egg is, however, itself something of an anomaly. If the general movement of the Universe is from order to disorder, how did the order (which presumably existed in the cosmic egg) originate? Where did it come from?

It is tempting to suppose that we can expand on the Biblical account for the answer. The Spirit of God, moving upon the face of the deep (Chaos), collected all the matter of the Universe into an ultimately compressed cosmic egg (Cosmos) and then allowed it to explode into energy ("Let there be light"), cool down into matter and the Universe as we know it, and then run downhill according to the laws of nature (presumably also designed by God) until it is Chaos again.

There is, however, no scientific evidence for that.

Nor is there any scientific evidence for any other form of creation for the cosmic egg.

If we study the distant galaxies, we are, in effect, studying the distant past, for the light of those galaxies took billions of years to reach us. However, even the farthest object we can detect existed after the big bang, and there seems to be no way of penetrating to a time before the big bang.

Yet there may be a way through what seems an absolute barrier to knowledge.

For instance, it may be that the Universe will not expand forever. It is expanding against the pull of its own gravitational field, which is constantly sapping the rate of expansion. It may be, then, that eventually the expansion will slow to a complete halt and that the Universe will make a slow turnabout and begin to contract again.

If so, it may be that the Universe, which is now winding down to chaos as it expands, will begin to wind up again as it contracts and will eventually form a new cosmic egg. Naturally, this should happen over and over again, and we should have an "oscillating Universe." In this case, there is no true beginning and no true ending; the Universe exists forever, with no problem as to where the infinite number of cosmic eggs came from or where the order came from.

Yet in order for the Universe to end its expansion, its gravitational field must be intense enough to bring about that end. The intensity of the Universe's gravitational field depends on the average density of matter in the Universe, and as nearly as scientists can now make out, the average density of the Universe is only about one one-hundredth of what it should be to enforce a stop in the expansion.

The evidence to that effect is not yet completely conclusive, and I have a hunch that the "missing mass" required to raise the density to the proper figure will yet be found and that the Universe will yet be discovered to oscillate. Experiments have been performed which seem to show that certain particles, called neutrinos, have a tiny mass. There are so many neutrinos in the Universe, however, that if the conclusions are correct, they may supply sufficient mass to bring about a contraction, and oscillation.

---

4 *And God saw the light, that it was good: and God divided* [17] *the light from the darkness.*

---

17. Light and darkness seem here to be viewed as opposite and, perhaps, equal phenomena that can be divided (that is, separated), each into its own domain.

This is a natural point of view for early man, who could not help but observe the alternation of day and night. It had to seem to people at the start that light ruled during the day and darkness during the night and that, on the whole, the time was divided equally between them.

This alternation and this equal division may have helped give rise to the thought that the Universe was a battlefield between the principle of Light and principle of Darkness, and that both had, perhaps, existed from the beginning and were equally powerful.

Light would be a symbolic representation of a god that reduces Chaos to Cosmos, while darkness is an anti-God that strives to turn Cosmos back into Chaos. (There is somehow a whisper of the Oscillating Universe here, where the Universe is formed out of a cosmic egg and then returns to a cosmic egg over and over. We might therefore imagine, if we had a very good imagination, that God's division of light from darkness marked the establishment of a period of expansion of the Universe and a period of contraction.)

The ancient Iranians worked out this notion of the battle between light and darkness in considerable detail. To them, the principle of light and good was Ahura-mazda, while the principle of darkness and evil was Ahriman. Both had an eternal and indestructible existence, and between them the Universe was created as a battlefield. The fight between them (and between immense armies of subordinate beings—angels and demons—on both sides, in which even human beings took part by the devotion of each to good or to evil) forever continues, though generally (perhaps out of wishful thinking) the mythologists assume that good is assured the final victory.

Eventually, when the Jews spent several centuries as part of the Persian Empire, this "dualism" entered their system of thought, and Satan arose as the equivalent of Ahriman, as the "anti-God" trying to negate the Creation.

The P-document, however, was put into writing during the Babylonian captivity, just before the Persian era, and Satan makes no appearance in it. Yet, although God is specifically described as creating light, he does not create the darkness, for darkness existed at the beginning, along with, and as part of, Chaos.

Nevertheless, since God can confine darkness by his word, he is as much master over it as over light, and dualism (the equal existence of principles of Good and Evil) is expressly denied.

From the scientific standpoint, of course, darkness does not have the same kind of existence as light; darkness is only the absence of light.

At the present stage of the Universe, with a billion trillion stars shining, there is light everywhere (with a few exceptions I will get to), and there is no darkness. To be sure, if one were at a spot in space between the galaxies, where even the nearest galaxies were so far away that the intensity of their light was dimmed by distance to a level indetectable by the human eye, one would be in darkness. That would be a subjective decision, however, for instruments more delicate than the eye could detect the light, so that one would not be in darkness at all, but only in excessively dim light.

Light might also be absent because it was physically blocked by an opaque barrier. On Earth we are accustomed to a far more intense level of light than we would be in the Universe generally, because of the closeness of one particular star, the sun. The level of light during the day, when we are on that portion of Earth's surface facing the sun, is so much higher than the level when the surface turns so as to face us away from the sun (with the bulk of the opaque Earth itself blocking its light) that we think of the night as representing darkness. If the sky is clear, however, there is the light of the stars and possibly of the moon, so it is not truly dark; it only seems so by comparison.

A cloudy night is darker still, and, of course, we reach the level of virtually zero light if we descend into a deep cave and make no use of artificial light.

The equivalent of a deep cave in open space would be the center of a cloud of dust and gas that does not include an actual star and is not too close to a star. Such clouds actually exist and are called dark nebulas. We can see them when they hide the stars behind them and appear as an area of blackness against a background of bright stars on all sides. If one were in the middle of such a cloud, there would be no light in the sky, only darkness.

Finally, if we imagine the Universe continuing to expand forever, there will come a time when all the stars will have ended their lives as glowing objects, when all will be dark in a final victory of Chaos.

But all these arguments in favor of the special cases in which darkness might exist depend on our narrow definition of light. In actuality, light is a wave phenomenon, the product of a rapidly oscillating electromagnetic field. The oscillation can take place with any period, and waves can be produced with any wavelength.

Our eye happens to be sensitive to certain wavelengths that our brain interprets as light. Those wavelengths make up only a small fraction of the whole, and there are wavelengths both longer and shorter that cannot be detected by our eyes and that do not appear as light.

All matter radiates these wavelengths in a wide range, the peak level being at some particular wavelength determined by its temperature. Matter not hot enough to produce wavelengths short enough to appear as light will produce longer wavelengths of infrared light or still longer wavelengths of microwaves or yet longer wavelengths of radio waves. To all of these we are not naturally sensitive, but we can detect them with appropriate instruments.

All matter that is not actually at absolute zero (and nothing is ever at absolute zero) produces such radiation. We could therefore detect infrared or radio-wave radiations in the deepest cave (since they would be radiated by the walls of the cave or by the air itself) or in the thickest and darkest cosmic cloud (since they would be radiated by the particles of matter in the cloud).

If we consider light as merely one representative, and the most easily noticed, of electromagnetic radiation, then, in a broader sense, there is no darkness anywhere in the Universe, no place anywhere and at any time, even during the ultimate chaos at the end, in which there is/ will be a complete absence of electromagnetic radiation.

Thus, it would seem that scientific conclusions are against the notion of light-dark dualism and are more in accord (at least metaphorically) with the Biblical notion of God ("light") as absolute master.

---

5 *And God called the light Day, and the darkness he called Night.*[18] *And the evening and the morning* [19] *were the first day.*[20]

---

18. God is described as giving the two phenomena of light and darkness specific names, Day and Night *(Yom* and *Lilah* in Hebrew).

This is in accord with the natural notion of most people that words have some natural existence, some objective meaning. To people who have never heard but one language it is always astonishing (even today) to come across anyone who cannot understand it. How can anyone fail to realize that something that is X is *called* X? It is even more astonishing to encounter another language in which every object, action, quality, and so on is called by apparently meaningless and nonsensical sounds that nevertheless convey meaning to others who speak the language.

The Biblical writers lived in a time when there were many languages, and they knew that fact. As most people do, they naturally assumed their own language, Hebrew, was a special one, the original one. Certainly, if we accept the Bible as literally true, then God speaks in the language in which the Bible was originally written. Hebrew becomes God's language.

It would seem from this verse that God created individual words and therefore the Hebrew language just as he created light. And he created language even before he created light, for the command to create light is put into Hebrew words.

It followed from this, and was assumed by Biblical writers (and by many later people who accepted the Bible literally), that Hebrew was the exclusive language of human beings well into historical times.

In actual fact, of course, languages have evolved in very complex fashion, and if there was any such thing as an original language, it is lost in the mists of time. Philologists can judge the past only from the relationships of present-day languages, and these can be carried back in time only as far as the writing of deciphered scripts exist. That takes us back only five thousand years at most, by which time languages were already numerous, complex, and vastly differentiated.

Nor is there anything unique, in the linguistic view, either in age or quality, about the Hebrew language or any of its words.

19. The twenty-four-hour period known as "day" offers us the possibility of confusion, since the lighted portion of that period is also known as "day" in contradistinction to "night," and is referred to as such in this very verse.

It is because of this possibility of confusion that the verse does not merely describe the creation of light and the separation of light and darkness as having occurred on the first day, but carefully refers to "the evening and the morning" to indicate that the full twenty-four-hour period is meant.

We moderns have the day (the twenty-four-hour period) begin and end at midnight, a convenient scheme, if a somewhat artificial one, which is made practical only because of the existence of clocks that are cheap enough to be in every household and accurate enough to give the time to the minute.

Before the days of cheap and accurate timepieces, it was much more natural (and, indeed, inevitable) to start the day either at sunrise or sunset, times that could be marked independently of clocks.

It might seem to us that of the two, sunrise and sunset, it is sunrise that marks the natural beginning of the day. It is certainly the beginning of the workday. It seems that in those portions of the Bible that reached their present form before the Babylonian captivity there are occasional indications that sunrise starts a new day.

Thus: "And the flesh of the sacrifice of his peace offerings for thanksgiving shall be eaten the same day that it is offered; he shall not leave any of it until the morning" (Leviticus 7:15). The "morning" is not the same day, apparently; it starts a new day.

It was the Babylonian system, however, to start the day at sunset, which meant the day began with evening and morning was the latter part of that same day. The writers of the P-document were influenced by this Babylonian custom and adopted it, so that they described the full twenty-four-hour day by saying, "the evening and the morning" rather than the reverse.

This custom of beginning the day at sunset continued into New Testament times and thus into some traditional holidays. "Christmas Eve" and "New Year's Eve" are by no means the evening *before* Christmas and New Year's. They are the *beginning* of Christmas and New Year's by Biblical tradition if not by the calendar or present-day recognition. In the same way Halloween ("All-Hallows Day eve") on October 31 is the first part of All-Hallows Day celebrated on November 1.

And of course the Jews still celebrate their holidays beginning at sunset of the "day before."

20. The acts of creation listed in the first chapter of Genesis are divided into separate "days."

Until the nineteenth century, there was never any question about this. It was universally assumed that the days referred to were literally days—twenty-four-hour periods—and that the heaven and the earth were created, and the job completed, in just a few of them. This did not seem to be overly short to anyone since God was involved. There was no question that if God had but willed it, the whole could have been created and completed in a few hours, or in an instant of time.

In the nineteenth century, however, it became more and more clear that Earth was millions of years old, and in almost the first retreat from the literal acceptance of the Bible, there began to be some hesitancy about those "days." Must they, after all, refer to a specific period of time?

Some Biblical scholars therefore began to wonder whether in this chapter day might not refer to some vague period, as though one were to say that the coming of light and its separation from darkness represented the "first stage" of the process of creation and that this stage might have lasted a million years, or a trillion, if God so willed it. What is time to God?

And yet the Bible seems to be specific. As though there were some chance that the word "day" might be misinterpreted, the P-document carefully states "the evening and the morning," as though to emphasize that it was one twenty-four-hour period and no more. The day referred to in this verse is still taken to be the familiar twenty-four-hour day and nothing more by Jewish and Christian fundamentalists today.

---

6 *And God said, Let there be a firmament* [21]
in the midst of the waters, and let it divide
the waters from the waters.[22]

---

21. The order in which God creates objects in the Universe during the remainder of this chapter is precisely the order in which the gods create them after the destruction of Tiamat in the Babylonian Creation-myths, some-

thing represented in the P-document by the creation of light and the subjection of darkness to limits.

First comes the creation of the firmament.

The first syllable of the word "firmament" is "firm," and that gives an accurate idea of what the writers of the P-document had in mind. The firmament is the semi-spherical arc of the sky (it looks flattened on top and rather semi-ellipsoidal, but that is an optical illusion), and it was considered a hard and firm covering of the flat earth. It was considered very much like the lid of a pot and was assumed to be of much the same material as an ordinary lid would be.

The word "firmament" (Latin *firmamentum*) is a translation of the Greek *stereoma*, which means "a hard object" and which is, in turn, a translation of the Hebrew *rakia*, meaning a thin metal plate.

From the scientific view, however, there is no firmament; no sky to be viewed as a material dome. What seems to be such to our eyes is merely space stretching out indefinitely.

There is, to be sure, an "end" to space. As our telescopes and other instruments penetrate farther and farther out into space, we can detect objects as far as twelve billion light-years away. Since the light from such distant objects left them twelve billion years ago, we see them as they were comparatively soon after the big bang.

We could see objects that were farther away still, but we do not. Apparently, if we penetrate further still into the past, we reach the stage where the Universe had not yet cooled off to the point where enough matter had settled out as galaxies and where enough energy had been converted into matter to let us see space as truly transparent. Beyond the last objects we can see, we see only the haze of the earliest primeval days after the big bang, and that, in a sense, represents the end (as well as the beginning of the Universe).

Clearly, though, this hazelike region that we cannot penetrate, which exists in every direction and which forms a sphere about us at a distance of more than twelve billion light-years, is not anything like what the priestly writers had in mind when they spoke of the firmament. It would take a metaphorical mind, indeed, to see the equivalence.

The Biblical firmament was not viewed by the early Jews as very far above Earth's surface. It had to clear Earth's mountains, of course, but it might very well not be much higher than that.

In the Greek myths, the giant Atlas had to support the sky as a kind of living pillar, and at one time, Hercules, by standing on a mountaintop, was able to take over the load temporarily—that seems to have been a typical ancient view of the sky, its distance and its solidity.

In the old legend of Jacob's dream, the sky could be reached by a ladder: "And he dreamed, and behold a ladder set up on the earth, and the top of it reached to heaven: and behold the angels of God ascending and descending on it" (Genesis 28:12).

22. Rain is essential to agriculture, as much to early man as to ourselves, and yet direct experience with rain was not always common. The early farmers who first made agriculture into a large-scale enterprise lived in the lowland valleys of great rivers in the Middle East—the Nile River in Egypt, the Tigris and Euphrates rivers in Iraq, and the Indus River in Pakistan.

Generally, these were not areas where it rained frequently (along the lower Nile it almost never rained). The rivers themselves supplied the water necessary for man, animals, and crops, and great effort had to be put into irrigation procedures to make sure that a good harvest could be achieved.

The river was fed by rains, yes, but those rains were likely to occur in the mountainous regions where the rivers originated, and the farmers near the mouth of the river had no direct experience with that.

When people from these dry farming civilizations did encounter rain, they were likely to be amazed at water falling from the sky—a kind of gift from the homes of the gods, since such falling water would water plants without the hard work of irrigation.

In those early days, then, it was natural for people to assume that there were two sources of water, the rivers

34

and the rain, which were separated from each other by the firmament.

---

7 *And God made* [23] *the firmament, and divided the waters which were under the firmament from the waters which were above the firmament:*[24] *and it was so.*

---

23. When God said, "Let there be light," there was instantly light, and that was that. However, light is an immaterial object, and human beings could see no way of fashioning it. The firmament is, however, a material object, at least in the view of ancient humanity, and therefore, after God says, "Let there be a firmament," the P-document goes on to say, "And God made the firmament."

This might be viewed as simply a restatement of the remark "Let there be a firmament," as indicating that God made the firmament merely by speaking the necessary words. On the other hand, it certainly gives the impression of God actually hammering out a thin metal shell, fitting it over Earth, and fastening it down.

That would be an unsophisticated way of looking at the Creation, but in the Babylonian Creation-myth, the gods seem to have fashioned the Universe in the human sense, and a little of that may have crept into the wording of the P-document.

This remnant of the Babylonian outlook might even explain why it was necessary to have God take days to do the job. If it were a matter of will alone, then the job could be done in an instant; if it were a matter of arduous metalwork, then it is an adequate indication of God's superhumanity that he could complete the entire sky in only one day.

24. Here is the direct indication that not only was there water below the firmament (the familiar water we encounter on the surface of Earth), but water above the firmament as well (the water that falls as rain).

35

It did not seem to occur to anyone to wonder whether the water supply above the firmament might someday be used up; or, for that matter, whether the water supply below the firmament might build up to the point where it would fill all the space available.

We now know, of course, that since there is no firmament in the Biblical sense, there are no waters above it. All the water that exists on Earth exists *on* Earth and nowhere else. The sun warms the ocean, producing water vapor, which precipitates as tiny water droplets, which gathers in clouds, which are blown by the wind, and which, under appropriate conditions, collect into larger drops and fall as rain, which then (if it falls on land) drains back into the ocean.

The entire cycle is an extremely complicated one and is hard to predict in detail (as any weather forecaster knows by experience), but it is a completely closed cycle, and the rain is as much "below the firmament" as the seas and rivers are.

---

8 *And God called the firmament Heaven.*[25]
And the evening and the morning were the second day.

---

25. Here is a clear indication that the first verse of Genesis is simply a summary of what is to follow. The first verse reads, "In the beginning God created the heaven and the earth," but, actually, "the heaven" is described as being created on the second day.

In this verse, "heaven" is specifically described as the name given to the firmament. Later in the Bible, it is occasionally used as a word for the dwelling place of God somewhere above the firmament. Thus: "The Lord is in his holy temple, the Lord's throne is in heaven" (Psalms 11:4).

Such a notion is found only in the latest-written portions of the Old Testament. Earlier, God was more likely to be thought of as living in Mt. Sinai or in the Ark of the Covenant. By New Testament times, however, the notion of a heaven as God's dwelling place above the firmament had become common so that the Lord's prayer begins: "Our Father which art in heaven" (Matthew 6:9).

Nowadays, when it is well understood that the firmament, in the Biblical sense, does not exist, Heaven is made use of solely as God's dwelling place, though that, too, plays no part in the Universe subject to scientific observation and measurement.

---

9 *And God said, Let the waters under the heaven be gathered together unto one place, and let the dry land appear:* [26] *and it was so.*

---

26. The order of the steps in the Creation as described in the first chapter of Genesis is an extremely logical one, given the scheme of things as seen by the writers of the P-document. Creation proceeds from the outside inward, so to speak, revolving in closer and closer to humanity, which is viewed as the climax of creation.

Thus, the conversion of Cosmos to Chaos by means of dividing and separating things, and thus putting an end to the random intermingling that is the mark of Chaos, begins on the first day with the creation of light and its separation from darkness. This deals with the immaterial.

On the second day, the material portion of the Universe is taken up, but only the part farthest removed from humanity: the sky overhead rather than the ground underfoot. The sky is used to separate part of the waters from the rest.

It is only on the third day that God turns to the earth itself, and again the act is one of separation. The earth is made up of water and land, chaotically mixed together, to begin with, in a sort of liquid mud (one would presume), but at the word of God, all the water is pushed to one side, while the land is packed together, dried out, and allowed to arise above sea level.

There is an interesting reverse similarity between this and the formation of Earth as science sees it.

About 4.6 billion years ago, Earth was forming through the coming together of larger and larger objects conglomerating out of the original cloud of dust and gas that formed the solar system. Just as the sun grew hotter and hotter as it absorbed the incoming energy of the parts that formed it, so did Earth.

Gathering far less matter than the sun did, Earth never grew as hot as the sun. It was hot enough, however, to possess neither atmosphere nor ocean to begin with. The light molecules that would have made up the atmosphere or ocean moved too quickly at Earth's high temperature to be held by its comparatively small gravitational field.

Yet some of the light molecules were held in more or less loose combination with other molecules that made up the solid substances of the forming Earth.

After Earth formed, the chaotic mixture of substances that composed it to begin with gradually settled out over some millions of years. The densest portions sank to Earth's center, where there is now a metal core, chiefly iron and nickel in a 10-to-1 ratio, that is mostly liquid because of the high temperatures.

The lighter rock rose to form Earth's mantle and crust. Little by little, natural geological processes forced the lightest molecules out of their loose combination with rock. Water collected and, being less dense than the rock, gradually rose and began to fill the lower basins of Earth's uneven surface. The still lighter molecules of gaseous substances bubbled up through rock and water to form an atmosphere.

Scientists are far from agreeing on the precise details of ocean formation, but it would seem the process resembles the Biblical account in reverse.

The Bible makes it seem that solid land appeared out of an initial liquid mass, but from the scientific view, it would seem that an ocean appeared out of an initial dry mass.

---

10 *And God called the dry land Earth; and the gathering together of the waters called he Seas: and God saw that it was good.*

11 *And God said, Let the earth bring forth grass,*[27] *the herb yielding seed, and the fruit tree yielding fruit after his kind,*[28] *whose seed is in itself, upon the earth: and it was so.*

---

27. As soon as the dry land appeared, God created plant life upon it. This may seem to us a little premature, since other forms of life were not to be created until later in the scheme of Creation.

In ancient times, however, plants were not considered to be alive in the same sense that animals were.

It wasn't till the 1830s, in fact, that scientific observations made it quite clear that plant and animal tissue were alike built up of cells; that both types of cells included the same general types of molecules and chemical reactions; and that both were equally alive.

To the writers of the P-document, however, the plant world was what the thinkers of the time supposed it to be—a food supply that it was the soil's innate property to produce.

In the scientific view of the beginnings of Earth, the first life to appear on dry land, some 425 million years ago, was indeed composed of various simple plants. It was perhaps only twenty million years later that animal life began to appear.

This is not surprising. The plants that appear on dry land are green because of their content of chlorophyll, which is capable of carrying through a process known as photosynthesis. The energy of visible light can be used, in photosynthesis, to split the water molecule into hydrogen and oxygen. The oxygen is released into the air, while the hydrogen is combined with the carbon dioxide of air to form starches, sugars, and fats. In combination with minerals absorbed from the soil, proteins, nucleic acids, and plant tissue generally are formed.

Animals cannot use the energy of visible light for this purpose. They can use the energy obtained only by oxidizing the molecules of plants (or of animals that have eaten plants).

Unless the plants have first trapped the energy of the sun to produce energy-containing substances, animals that depend upon those energy-containing substances cannot live.

Therefore it is plants first—followed inevitably by animals. The two types of life, existing together, keep things in balance. Plants consume carbon dioxide and water to form oxygen and complicated molecules, while animals consume the complicated molecules and oxygen to form carbon dioxide and water. The cycle is powered by the energy of sunlight.

28. The emphasis here of herb yielding seed and fruit tree yielding fruit "after his kind" seems to mean that the apple tree, for instance, will produce more apple trees and nothing else; that carrots will produce more carrots and nothing else; and so on.

This is one of the verses that seem to indicate that life was divided into separate species at the very start and that there is no way in which one species can turn into another.

With this, the scientific view is in thorough disagreement. The fossil evidence, as well as genetic, biochemical, and physiological evidence, all agree that life developed slowly over billions of years, one species differentiating into two or more, and many dying out altogether, in a process termed biological evolution.

While no scientific conclusion is, or can be, completely certain, the evidence in favor of evolution is so strong that no reputable biologist doubts the fact, however much uncertainty there may be over the fine details.

---

12 *And the earth brought forth grass, and herb yielding seed after his kind, and the tree yielding fruit, whose seed was in itself, after his kind: and God saw that it was good.*

13 *And the evening and the morning were the third day.*

14 *And God said, Let there be lights* [29] *in the firmament of the heaven to divide the day from the night;* [30] *and let them be for signs, and for seasons, and for days, and years;* [31]

---

29. With dry land formed, God made the final adjustment to the sky in preparation for the creation of animal life. The "lights" he created are the various glowing objects in the sky: the sun, the moon, the planets, and the stars.

Light was already created on the first day, but the light-giving objects in the heaven were created only on the fourth day. This is not necessarily a contradiction, since it is quite easy to see that neither the sun nor any other heavenly body might have been essential to the production of light according to the Biblical view. Light could be viewed as an immaterial essence and the sun as merely its container.

During the first three days of Biblical Creation, we might imagine the sky to be full of a diffuse light that would amply illuminate Earth. The creation of the "lights in the firmament" would then represent the collection of that light into a limited area.

This has, in fact, an interesting correspondence to the scientific view of the creation of the Universe. If we consider the "Let there be light" command to represent the big bang, then, for a period of time after that, light (or, more generally, energy) existed diffusely through the entire Universe. (The Universe was, of course, far smaller in its early days than it is now.)

It took quite a while (as time is counted in human terms) for the energy concentration to cool off and for the forming matter to collect into galaxies and stars. From that viewpoint, "the lights in the firmament" *were* created after light itself.

30. In the continuing process of converting Chaos to Cosmos, God goes on with his process of separation and division. By collecting the primordial diffuse light and

packing it into various containers, and by placing almost all of it into the sun, he brought about a more efficient separation of light and darkness, of day and night than would have been possible when that separation was decreed on the first day.

31. The "lights in the firmament" have several uses; the first one commented on is that they be "for signs, and for seasons, and for days, and years."

Even in early prehistoric times, the movements of the heavenly bodies served to indicate time. The movements of the sun marked off the alternations of day and night. The movements of the moon marked off the months and years. The particular constellations in the sky at a particular time of night marked off the seasons of the year.

All this is very important to farmers, herdsmen, and hunters, since the burgeoning and dying of plants, the mating and bearing of domestic animals, and the migrations of wild animals are all seasonal phenomena. But if we accept the importance of seasons, days, and years, what is meant by "signs"?

The word "signs" may not be on a par with the other three terms, and the placing of it on a par may be a fault in the King James translation. In The New English Bible, the verse is made to read "and let them serve as signs both for festivals and for seasons and for years," thus giving "signs" the significance of "a calendar."

And yet . . .

The word "sign" is most often used in the Bible to signify a miraculous deed of God designed to warn human beings of the path they must take. When Moses is sent to Pharaoh to direct him to free the Israelite slaves, God gives Moses the power to produce two different miracles designed to impress the Israelites and to persuade them to follow his leadership. God says, "And it shall come to pass, if they will not believe thee, neither hearken to the voice of the first sign, that they will believe the voice of the latter sign" (Exodus 4:8).

Later, when God promises Moses the ability to perform additional miracles, he says, "And thou shalt take this rod in thine hand, wherewith thou shalt do signs" (Exodus 4:17).

With reference to the plagues that will visit Egypt as an indication of the displeasure of God and a warning to Pharaoh to obey the dictates of Moses, ". . . I will . . . multiply my signs and my wonders in the land of Egypt" (Exodus 7:3).

It is clear that a "sign," then, is some deed of God intended to give notice to human beings, to direct them, to punish them. The heavenly bodies would then be described as existing not only for the purpose of establishing a calendar, but as offering a method for determining the will of God.

As it happens, the various peoples who inhabited the Tigris-Euphrates valley (whom we may lump together as the Babylonians) were the first to work out in some detail the motion of the planets against the background of the stars, and remained the most advanced in this respect right down to the period of the Jewish captivity in the sixth century B.C.

The shiftings of position on the part of the sun, the moon, and the five known planets (Mercury, Venus, Mars, Jupiter, and Saturn) were complex, and the Babylonians assumed the complexity was there for a purpose. Since they further assumed that everything about the Universe was made for the use of humanity (something the Bible assumes as well), then this complexity must have some meaning *for man.*

The Babylonians deified the planets (something picked up by other people and retained even by us to the extent that we still give the planets the names of Roman and Greek gods), and so it was easy for them to suppose that the complex movements of the planets represented hidden messages from the gods, designed to guide humanity. The movements were a cryptogram revealing the plans of the gods and therefore serving as a searchlight into the future. The Universe could be made less willful and humanity more secure if human beings could somehow learn to interpret the cosmic code.

The Babylonians labored to interpret the code from the shapes they imagined the constellations to represent, from the symbolism they saw fit to apply to each planet, and from other deductions it seemed to them to be sensible to make.

In short, the Babylonians were the first to invent a complicated system of what we now call astrology, something that was passed on to the Greeks and Romans and through them to medieval and modern Europe.

The Jewish exiles in Babylonia scorned the Babylonian religion, and even when they adopted the general brush-strokes of the Babylonian Creation-myth, they modified it to remove what was found most offensive. Thus, the plurality of Babylonian gods were removed in favor of one transcendent God; any hint of a rival of God or of danger from the forces of Chaos is removed; and so on.

The Jews disapproved of the deification of the heavenly bodies, and in their Creation account, they stated specifically that the heavenly bodies were created by God and were therefore helplessly subject to his will.

Since Babylonian astrology rested strongly on Babylonian polytheism, the Jews scorned that, too. They were sure that God guided mankind, but they preferred to believe he did so by dreams or by direct communication, rather than through some mysterious code in the sky for anyone to read—or fail to read.

Nevertheless, the one word "signs" enters into this verse, and it is tempting to suppose that it may be a reference to astrology that was somehow included and, once it was, became too sacred to remove.

The scientific view of the Universe holds astrology to be a useless superstition. Whether a planet is here or there in the sky cannot possibly affect the character and personality of individuals born at this particular time or that, nor can it guide them in their daily activities.

---

15 *And let them be for lights in the firmament of the heaven to give light upon the earth:* [32] *and it was so.*

---

32. The use of the "lights" to give light is mentioned only after their use for calendar-forming purposes. To us, it would seem that the light-giving purpose is primary, but that would not fit in with the internal logic of the P-document.

The diffuse light of the first three days would have been quite ample to give light to humanity. From that diffuse light, however, steady and unchanging, there would have been no way of measuring time. The sun, the moon, the planets, and stars, by shifting their positions relative to each other, make a calendar possible, but the fact that they also give light is secondary.

---

16 *And God made two great lights;* [33] *the greater light* [34] *to rule the day,* [35] *and the lesser light to rule the night:* [36] *he made the stars also.* [37]

---

33. The two great lights are, of course, the sun and the moon. They are clearly larger than any of the planets or stars. They are the only glowing objects in the sky (barring an occasional comet, and comets are never mentioned in the Bible) that show up as something more than mere dots of light.

Incidentally, although God is described on the first day as naming Day and Night, and on the second day as naming Earth and Sea, he is not described as naming the sun and the moon, which are referred to in these verses only as "lights." To be sure, there is no chance of misinterpretation as to what the P-document means, but neither was there any chance of misinterpretation in the earlier cases.

34. The sun is the greater light, but not in actual apparent size. The sun and the moon are almost exactly equal in apparent size, as can be seen whenever the moon moves in front of the sun to produce a total solar eclipse.

That this is so is entirely coincidence. The moon and sun are of course quite different in size. The moon has a diameter of 2,160 miles, and the sun one of 864,000 miles, but the sun is just sufficiently far away to cancel out its greater size. There is nothing in the laws of nature to make that necessary; it is just chance.

As far as the intensity of light delivered is concerned, there is no question that the sun is the "greater light." It yields 465,000 times as much light as does the moon at its brightest. The reason is not hard to find. The sun is an extremely hot body that shines of its own light. The moon shines only by what small fraction of that light it can catch and reflect.

35. The sun is described as ruling over the day. Day and night had been created and named, in the Biblical account, on the first day of Creation. Presumably, the diffuse primordial light brightened the heaven for part of the time and did not do so the rest of the time, so that there was day and night *without* the sun.

Once the diffuse light was collected into the sun, however, the light waxed and waned with the sun's height in the sky and quickly faded to extinction after the sun had left the sky. In that sense the sun ruled the day.

In the scientific view, however, there is nothing that is analogous to a diffuse light in the sky that shines only part of the time. What's more, the sun does not merely rule the day (as though day had some existence independently of the sun); it *is* the day. What we call day is the result of our being near a source of light as bright as the sun is. If the sun did not exist, neither would day.

36. The lesser light, or the moon, rules the night in that it is the most prominent feat of the night sky—when it is there at all. The moon, however, follows an apparent path across the sky that is independent of the sun's apparent path. This means that at any given moment it is as likely to be in the sky when the sun is in the sky as when the sun is not in the sky.

Nevertheless, the sun's brilliance pales the moon when it is present, so that the moon is not noticeable in the day sky. And except for a night or two every twenty-nine or thirty days, when the moon is shining very close to the sun indeed (on rare occasions, so close as to move in front of it), the moon is visible in the night sky at some time, even if only for a short period just after sunset or just before dawn. And whenever it is in the night sky, it is the most noticeable object in it.

An added factor to the moon's noticeability is that unlike the sun it is not always and invariably a circle of light, but goes through a series of "phases" instead. From night to night it changes, beginning as a thin crescent just after sunset, gradually waxing as it moves farther from the sun in the sky, until it is a full moon, a perfect circle of light high in the sky at midnight, then waning again until it is a thin crescent just before the dawn. It then moves past the sun from west to east and begins the cycle over again. (In general, the more the moon waxes and the brighter it gets, the greater the fraction of the night it can be seen shining in the sky, till at full moon it is in the sky all night long.)

For all these reasons, it is fair to associate the moon with the night rather than with the day, even if it does spend as much time in the day sky as in the night sky.

The phases of the moon were fundamental to early calendars, which began a new month at each new moon (the first appearance of the crescent just after sunset). The Babylonians did this, and the Jews and Greeks copied them.

37. The stars are dismissed quickly, almost as an afterthought. It was necessary to mention them, to make them clearly a creation of God and not divine in their own right, but since they played no direct part in either giving light or in setting up a calendar, they required no more than a few words. The starlike planets—Mercury, Venus, Mars, Jupiter, and Saturn—are not given any special mention.

The P-document makes it clear that Earth is older than any of the heavenly bodies. Earth was rescued from Chaos, and the dry land (with its plant cover) was created on the third day. The heavenly bodies were then created, at a stroke, on the fourth day.

The scientific view is quite different. The formation of the solar system out of the original cloud was of such a nature that all its bodies were formed at essentially the same time. The sun, the moon, Earth, and all the planets, satellites, asteroids, and comets are essentially the same age; each one is about 4.6 billion years old. Earth is not older than the sun or the moon.

As for the stars, they are of varying age, some being older, even considerably older, than the sun and Earth. Some stars must be just about as old as the Universe, having been formed comparatively soon after the big bang and are, perhaps, three times the age of the sun and Earth.

---

17 *And God set them in the firmament of the heaven to give light upon the earth,*

18 *And to rule over the day and over the night, and to divide the light from the darkness: and God saw that it was good.*

19 *And the evening and the morning were the fourth day.*

20 *And God said, Let the waters bring forth abundantly the moving creature* [38] *that hath life,* [39] *and fowl that may fly above the earth* [40] *in the open firmament of heaven.*

---

38. Now that all the nonliving paraphernalia of heaven and earth have been formed, it is time to produce that which represents the climax of Creation—life.

In the case of life, too, matter proceeds by stages to the peak of climax. Since that will be humanity, which lives on land, God first forms those portions of life that do not inhabit land, but that are characteristic of the sea and air.

First the sea is mentioned. The creation is that of "the moving creature"; that is, animal life, as contrasted with the rooted plants, which do not change their place and which were formed on the third day.

39. The moving creatures of the sea are specifically mentioned as being alive ("that hath life"), something that was not done in connection with the land vegetation

created on the third day. Here is clear evidence that, in the view of the P-document, the plant world is not truly alive, that land plants existed before animals of any kind, and that the creation of life began only on the fifth day.

According to the scientific view, animal life *did* exist in the sea before it existed on land, as the Bible indicates, but in opposition to the order in the P-document, plants (which are also alive) *also* existed in the sea before they existed on land.

In fact, for some three billion years, the sea contained life while the land was sterile. The most primitive forms of life were tiny cells the size of bacteria that were neither truly plant nor animal by today's criteria. Some of these cells (the "blue-green algae") possessed chlorophyll and could carry through photosynthesis—they were plantlike in that respect.

Even today, the ocean is full of microscopic life on which the larger and more complicated forms feed. Much of this floating microscopic life ("plankton") consists of green-plant cells that photosynthesize precisely as the green plants of the land do.

The sea is as filled with vegetation as the land is, and this sea vegetation provides some four-fifths of all the photosynthesis on Earth.

However, whereas the land vegetation is large enough to be seen with the unaided eye and is, indeed, in the case of most trees, larger and taller than any animals, the sea vegetation (except for seaweed) is invisible. Consequently, the P-document, which describes the creation of land vegetation, ignores sea vegetation altogether.

The early microscopic life also included animal cells, which could not perform photosynthesis and which lived on plant cells. It wasn't till about six hundred million years ago that good-sized multicellular animals evolved, animals possessing sufficiently complex structures to leave noticeable fossil remains behind.

Complex animal life in the sea existed for nearly two hundred million years before land vegetation appeared, a reverse of the order presented in the P-document.

It was not till about 425 million years ago that plants evolved structures and functions that made it possible to live on dry land, with animals following soon after.

40. The word "fowl" can be used for the common rooster and hen, specifically; for any large edible bird, more generally; and for any bird at all, still more generally. "Fowl" is related to the German *Vogel,* which means "bird." The Hebrew word *oph* translated in the King James Version as "fowl" is more accurately translated (in modern terms) as "bird" in the Revised Standard Version.

In fact, *oph* has a more general meaning still, for birds are by no means the only animals capable of flight. There are the bats, which are mammals but which have the full power of flight. On the basis of their flying, the Biblical writers include them with the birds. Thus, when the Bible lists those birds that may not be eaten, one verse reads, "And the stork, the heron after her kind, and the lapwing, and the bat" (Leviticus 11:19).

It amuses some moderns that the Biblical writers classify bats with birds or, for that matter, whales with fish. To us, bats and whales are mammals, even though the former can fly and the latter never leave the sea.

All classifications, however, are man-made. We group certain animals as mammals for various physiological reasons—such as bearing live young, possessing milk glands and a diaphragm, having hair, and so on. This makes particular sense in the light of the evolutionary development of life.

It may, however, be convenient to make other classifications. Whales may be more like rabbits, physiologically, than they are like fish. Still, if you want to catch whales, you have to go where the fish are and not where the rabbits are. In a practical sense, then, it could be useful to classify on the basis of habitat, placing whales with fish and bats with birds.

You might even classify insects with birds, as the Bible actually does, since insects also fly. In listing the living creatures that might not be eaten, the Bible says, "All fowls that creep, going upon all four, shall be an abomination unto you" (Leviticus 11:20). Since the very next two verses make an exception in the case of locusts, which leap rather than creep, it seems clear that by "all fowls that creep" is meant insects. The Revised Standard Version, in this verse, speaks of "winged insects" rather than "fowl."

The Hebrew *oph,* then, refers to three very different kinds of flying creatures: insects, birds, and bats. (There would also have been a fourth kind—the flying reptiles called pterosaurs—had they not been so long extinct that the Biblical writers knew nothing of them.)

In the P-document, all flying creatures were created at once at a single command, but in the scientific view, they came into being separately and at very long intervals.

The oldest of the flying creatures are the insects. Primitive insects are among the first animals to colonize the land surfaces of Earth about four hundred million years ago. Those first insects were probably flightless, however, and it may not have been till three hundred million years ago that the first flying insects evolved.

For over a hundred million years, the air belonged to insects alone. Then, about one hundred seventy million years ago, the first pterosaurs and birds evolved.

About seventy million years ago, the pterosaurs became extinct, but both insects and birds survived and continued to flourish.

Bats were the last of the flyers, having evolved only about fifty million years ago.

---

21 *And God created great whales,*[41] *and every living creature that moveth, which the waters brought forth abundantly, after their kind,*[42] *and every winged fowl after his kind: and God saw that it was good.*

---

41. The word given as "whale" in the King James Version is *tannin* in the Hebrew, and what it actually means is "a great fish of the sea." *Tannin* is translated as "sea-monster" in the Revised Standard Version.

51

Elsewhere in the Bible, *tannin* is used for living things that are clearly not whales. Thus, God tells Moses, ". . . Take thy rod, and cast it before Pharaoh, and it shall become a serpent" (Exodus 7:9). It is also used when God is addressed thus: ". . . thou brakest the heads of the dragons in the waters" (Psalm 74:13).

The *tannin* referred to in this portion of the Creation-myth may hark back to the sea monster of Chaos in the Babylonian Creation-myth. The specific mention of "great whales" may, then, really be a way of indicating that the sea monsters spoken of by the Babylonians are by no means anti-gods that can fight with God even on the off-chance of winning. Even the largest monstrous example of life is, like everything else, but a creation of God and is utterly subject to him.

Of course, a sea monster is exactly what whales are. The blue whale of Antarctic waters can be as much as one hundred feet long and weigh as much as one hundred fifty tons. It is not only the largest living animal, but is probably the largest animal that has ever lived on Earth.

Not quite as large is the sperm whale, which can attain lengths of seventy feet. It is the most formidable of the whales, however, and is ferocious and carnivorous, whereas the blue whale feeds only on tiny creatures. Other examples of large and monstrous sea creatures are various giant sharks, giant squids, giant jellyfish, giant crocodiles, giant clams, and so on. As examples of extinct giants of the past, there were the plesiosaurs, huge sea reptiles with lengths (mostly neck) of nearly fifty feet.

The Bible also contains reference to "leviathan," which in various places may refer to real animals such as crocodiles and serpents, but can also refer to the sea monster of Chaos as "Thou brakest the heads of leviathan in pieces . . ." (Psalm 74:14).

In later legends invented by rabbinical romancers, leviathan became an impossibly huge monster, based on the rather poetic description in the forty-first chapter of the Book of Job, where, in prosaic fact, the reference is probably to the crocodile.

In this verse, it would seem that all creatures of the sea were created simultaneously. According to the scientific view, on the other hand, this is far from being the case.

The first microscopic forms of sea life came into being about three and one-half billion years ago. Sizable invertebrate forms swarmed in the sea about six hundred million years ago, while the earliest known fish appeared about five hundred million years ago.

About two hundred million years ago, the plesiosaurs evolved; they became extinct about seventy million years ago.

The cetaceans (that is, the whales, dolphins, and porpoises) are mammals and undoubtedly had land-living ancestors, though we don't have the evidence for their evolution and can't identify their ancestors. They first appeared in the sea about seventy million years ago.

42. The animals, like the plants, are described as having been created in separate species ("after their kind"). Once again, this is not the scientific view, which regards all species of animals as having evolved from previous somewhat different species, back to the first primordial bit of life—formed by random processes.

---

22 *And God blessed* [43] *them, saying, Be fruitful and multiply,* [44] *and fill the waters in the seas, and let fowl multiply in the earth.* [45]

---

43. To "bless" is to confer felicity, prosperity, good fortune. Properly, only God can bless, since only he can control fate. Human beings can, however, call down blessings in God's name, and, presumably, God can heed them or not as he pleases.

44. The first occasion on which God confers a blessing is in his command that the animals of the sea and air "Be fruitful and multiply."

This makes sense, since living things cannot multiply their numbers unless they have ample food and a secure environment; and ample food and a secure environment are certainly felicity, as anyone who has gone without one or the other would testify.

According to the P-document, however, the blessing is given at the very beginning of life, and it is possible that God created only limited numbers of each species or even that he created only one pair of each species. To be sure, the preceding verse says that "the waters brought forth abundantly," but that may mean that many different species of sea life were created and not necessarily that many individuals of each species were created. We might argue, then, that there was a largely empty world into which to expand and that the command to be fruitful and multiply made much sense.

What is a blessing under one condition, however, may not be a blessing under others. After a dry spell, there can be no blessing like a steady, soaking rain. But when the rivers are flooding, a day of steady, soaking rain is not a blessing but a curse.

In the same way, it has been frequently found among animals that overmultiplication during brief periods of unusually favorable conditions can lead to an overconsumption of food, which will in turn lead, when conditions become less favorable, to famine, to disease, and to a plunge in numbers well below the level that had been supported before the brief period of unusually favorable conditions. This is an example of the command "Be fruitful and multiply" turning into a curse.

Demographers—those who study population dynamics—have long known that the command "Be fruitful and multiply" has become an increasingly dubious blessing as far as human beings are concerned.

In 1798, the English economist Thomas Robert Malthus first pointed out the dire consequences of overpopulation. He held that the capacity for human multiplication was such that human numbers were bound to outstrip the human food supply and that war, famine, and disease were all nature's ways of canceling out the overgreat tendency for humanity to multiply. The only way out of a dreary and never-ending round of catastrophe, then, he said, was to produce fewer children by sexual abstinence. (A forlorn hope, if that is the only way out.)

Malthus's gloom seemed to be misplaced, for even as

he wrote, the world was beginning the Industrial Revolution, which enabled humanity to make use of inanimate sources of energy (coal, oil, natural gas, moving water and wind, and so on) to increase greatly the food-yield of the world. In addition, science greatly increased the security of life against such things as disease, improper diet, and other threats.

This was merely a postponement, however, and not at all an abolition of the danger. The population of Earth is now more than four times what it was in Malthus's time, and on the average, people live better. The expenditure of energy that has made all this possible, it should be remembered, is at a rate hundreds of times as great as in Malthus's time. We are beginning to have trouble maintaining the supply of energy required to keep the world moving smoothly, and the total population is now putting an unbearable strain on the world's ecological balance.

Under these circumstances, every further increase in population is an enormous danger, and the primal command, "Be fruitful and multiply," has become, under changed circumstances, not a blessing but a deadly curse.

45. The command to multiply is given only to animals. There had been no such blessing given to the world of plants when it was created on the third day. That would appear to be because each plant seems to produce seed of itself.

Animals, on the other hand, clearly had to pair off and engage in sexual activity to produce young. The blessing was needed in the case of animals, therefore, to give them the necessary inspiration and vigor for coupling.

Yet plants, too, have both male and female sex cells. If the plants themselves cannot move, the grains of pollen, which carry the male sex cells, can be carried to the pistil at the center of a flower by the wind or by the unwitting action of insects or birds. (The pistil contains the female sex cells.)

Many plants have both pistils and pollen-producing anthers in each blossom. Pollen from the anthers can fertilize the pistil in the same blossom (self-fertilization) in some plants. In other plants, however, fertilization will work only if pollen from one plant reaches the pistil of another plant of the same species (cross-fertilization).

In some species of plants, in fact, some individual plants produce only the male sex cells and others only the female sex cells; in those cases, then, we have male and female plants. This was first pointed out by the Italian botanist Prospero Alpini about 1600, and it created quite a furor among those who were sure, on the basis of their interpretation of the Bible, that plants were fundamentally different from animals in such things.

---

23 *And the evening and the morning were the fifth day.*

24 *And God said, Let the earth bring forth the living creature after his kind,[46] cattle,[47] and creeping thing,[48] and beast of the earth [49] after his kind: and it was so.*

---

46. With the animals of the sea and air created, God turns to the final and (from the human point of view) most important habitat, the land. Here, too, animals are created all at once in separate species according to the Biblical account, and here, too, the scientific view insists on creation by the long, slow process of evolution.

47. The word "cattle" is from the Latin word for "property" (so is the related word "capital"). In early herding societies, the chief form of wealth was in the herds of animals such as kine, sheep, goats, swine, camels, horses, donkeys, and mules.

The word has come to be restricted to kine (bulls and cows) to such an extent that the word "kine" has become obsolete. In this verse, however, it would seem best to take "cattle" as meaning domesticated mammals or, at least, mammals capable of domestication, as distinguished from wild animals.

It might be assumed from this verse that some mammals were created domesticated from the start, but that, of course, is not so. All animals were wild to begin with, and domestication was an arduous procedure that took place comparatively late in human history.

48. The "creeping thing" here refers to all nonflying nonmammals. Chiefly, this means reptiles (a term that itself comes from the Latin word meaning "to creep") such as snakes and lizards. It would also include land amphibia, such as toads, and land invertebrates that do not fly, such as snails, spiders, worms, and so on.

49. By "beast of the earth" is meant the wild mammals, generally.

Actually, the mammals did not appear on Earth at the same time as other land-living organisms. Animals first colonized the dry land about four hundred million years ago, and to begin with, they were invertebrates and amphibia.

Not until about one hundred eighty million years ago did the first mammals appear; they were small and primitive varieties resembling the opossum more than any other present-day mammals.

Mammals didn't really come into their own till the giant reptiles became extinct seventy million years ago, and they didn't become the recognizable mammals of today till about thirty-five million years ago.

---

25 *And God made the beast of the earth after his kind, and cattle after their kind, and every thing that creepeth upon the earth after his kind: and God saw that it was good.*

26 *And God said, Let us [50] make man [51] in our image, after our likeness:[52] and let them have dominion over the fish of the sea, and over the fowl of the air, and over the cattle, and over all the earth, and over every creeping thing that creepeth upon the earth.[53]*

---

50. God is now ready for the final, climactic act of the Creation. It is still the sixth day, the one on which the land animals are created, but there is still a land-living creature remaining to be formed who is not, in the eyes of the Biblical writers, an animal but is something infinitely more.

The magnitude of this final act is such that God, who, till now, has been pictured as issuing his commands with instant decision, is pictured (however briefly) taking counsel, as though, for this one thing, he can use advice.

The phrase "Let us" certainly sounds as though God is addressing someone, as though more than one entity is involved. In the Babylonian Creation-myth, which the P-document adapts, there was indeed more than one entity involved; there were numerous gods, and as a matter of fact, the word "God" in the P-document is the translation of the Hebrew *Elohim*, which is the *plural* form for the Hebrew word for God and should, properly, be translated as "gods."

Since a polytheistic interpretation of the Creation-tale of the P-document is unthinkable to those who accept the Bible as a holy book, alternate explanations have been offered. The phrase "let us," instead of "let me" (and, later in the verse, the use of "our" instead of "my") has been explained as the use of the royal "we" or the editorial "we," a term that indicates majesty or that deliberately seeks to suppress individuality. However, such uses of the first-person plural are comparatively recent inventions and weren't known in Biblical times.

It might be argued that the plural is used in reference to the vast multiplicity of power and attributes of an infinite deity, so that the use of the singular is inappropriate. This, however, verges too close to an admission of polytheism.

Another possibility is that God is here addressing the angels. It might be that in the ages before the first verse of the Bible, God had created a heavenly state with an angelic court, and that the Creation as described in the P-document was carried through with the cooperation of angels or, at the very least, for the delectation of the angels, who form an admiring audience. In that case, this final "let us" is to call their attention to the particular virtuosity of the final act of creation and make sure that none of them miss it by allowing their attention to wander at the crucial moment.

However, the notion of a multiplicity of angels as constituents of a heavenly court is a rather late development in Jewish thinking. It arose during the period when the Jews formed part of the Persian Empire, with its dualistic philosophy of the cosmos. At the time the P-document came to be in its present form, the Persian influence had not yet made itself felt.

To Christians, who consider God to be a Trinity of three co-equal aspects—Father, Son, and Holy Spirit—the "let us" might be viewed as the three aspects of the Trinity communing among themselves. This is an interesting thought, which would explain the verse neatly, but there is no sign anywhere in the Old Testament that the Jews accepted the notion of a Trinity.

The most straightforward explanation arises from the fact that, as far as we know, primitive religion has always been polytheistic in nature. It has always seemed to primitive peoples that every different natural phenomenon requires a different deity.

The first person we know of who seemed to think that a single God could wield the power necessary to control and guide all earthly phenomena was the Egyptian Pharaoh Amenhotep IV, who took the name Ikhnaton and who reigned from 1385 to 1358 B.C. His attempted religious reformation did not, however, long outlive his death.

The tribes of Israel in their early days were probably also polytheists, and the monotheists among them (always a minority until the Babylonian captivity) struggled for centuries to impose their views on the rest of the nation without much success. The Bible indicates that well enough.

By the time the Bible was written down in its present form, however, the writers were staunch monotheists, and the history of Israel was retold from a monotheist point of view.

The legends preceding known history were also revised to reflect the monotheist point of view, and this wasn't always easy. Some of the tales and legends were very familiar in their polytheistic form, and some turns of phrase were too well known to be altered.

Thus, the Israelites and all the surrounding people, including the Egyptians and the nations of the Tigris-Euphrates valley, would speak of "the gods" rather than of "God"; that is, in Hebrew, of *Elohim* rather than *El*. *Elohim* became such a familiar term that it became inseparable from the deity, and when the priestly writers imposed a strictly monotheistic interpretation on their version of the Babylonian Creation-myth, they still had to keep the plural *Elohim* for the singular deity.

This would also account for the use of "Let us" and "our." The terms were too familiar to change even though they harked back to an earlier and an inadmissible state of polytheism.

51. The word "man" is a translation of the Hebrew word *adam*. The word *adam* is not really a proper name, though it came to be used as one.

The formation of human beings is here described as the last act of Creation; from the scientific viewpoint, this is not very far wrong.

The first primates, the broad group of mammals that includes the human species, evolved about seventy million years ago, not long after the extinction of the dinosaurs. It was not till forty million years ago that there evolved a tailless primate of a type we might recognize as an ape.

Perhaps twenty million years ago, the first species evolved that resembled modern human beings somewhat more than it resembled modern apes—this species was the first "hominid."

It was not till a mere two million years ago that the first species evolved that was sufficiently like modern human beings to be put in the same genus: "Homo." This was *Homo habilis,* whose brain, while considerably smaller than yours or mine, was already larger than that of any ape living, either then or now.

About one hundred fifty thousand years ago, the first

specimens of *Homo sapiens* appeared. Those oldest forms of our species are commonly known as Neanderthal men. The bony structure of the Neanderthal skeleton differs from ours in ways that, while minor, are noticeable.

Finally, by fifty thousand years ago, "modern man" appeared; human beings like ourselves in every particular.

Modern man, then, has existed for 1/1400 of the time that primates in general have existed; 1/70,000 of the time that life as a whole has existed on Earth; less than 1/90,000 of the time that the Earth has existed; and about 1/300,000 of the time the Universe has existed.

52. The phrase "in our image, after our likeness" is usually interpreted, these days, as meaning that God intends to give humanity the power of reason, or the power of ethical judgment, or the possession of an immortal soul, or the capacity to grasp the existence of and to worship God—all of these qualities being similar to attributes possessed by God and none of these qualities being possessed by any other form of life.

In all early forms of religion, however, deities are pictured very often in human shape, though sometimes in animal shape and sometimes in a mixture of animal and human.

The best examples of representations of deities that we know in our present Western culture are the statues of the gods formed by the Greeks. These are not only clearly human but extraordinarily good-looking as well, as one might expect.

It doesn't take much risk to suppose that the early Israelites, like all the surrounding peoples, thought of divine beings as human in shape, though some of the features of animals might be added as well. (Even today, we generally picture angels as human beings in nightgowns with large bird wings attached.)

If we think of God today, we are very likely to think of him as human in appearance—rather like Michelangelo's picture of God on the ceiling of the Sistine Chapel—a stern patriarch with a long white beard.

It could well be, then, that the writers of the P-document, in composing this phrase, meant it literally. They viewed God as possessing a human appearance, though, of course, one that is supernaturally brilliant and handsome. Human beings, shaped after God's form, are in this way distinct from all other forms of life.

In the scientific view, of course, there is no distinction of any importance between human beings and other forms of life. The human being is made up of cells just as all other forms of life are, right down to the bacteria. The key molecules making up the human being are the nucleic acids and proteins, which make up all other forms of life without exception, even down to the subcellular viruses.

Physiologically, the human being resembles other mammals just as much as other mammals resemble each other, and our species clearly belongs to the order of primates. Furthermore, the resemblances between the human being, on the one hand, and the chimpanzee and the gorilla, on the other, are so detailed, right down to the minutest point of physiology and biochemistry, that the real puzzle is that the small differences that do exist are sufficient to produce three different species.

The course of evolution, insofar as it explains the formation of all the species of life, also explains the formation of *Homo sapiens*. There are no added features to the evolutionary account, not one, that must be added to account for the human being.

The only difference between ourselves and the other animals worth mentioning is that we have an extraordinarily large brain for our size and an extraordinary supple pair of hands. The amount by which we exceed the chimpanzee and gorilla in this respect is sufficient to account for our science, art, philosophy, and philanthropy—to say nothing of our crimes and follies.

53. Human beings at the present time clearly dominate the earth and most of its life forms. In the Biblical account this is so from the start, and by divine fiat. Human beings were created in order to be master, and the other living things, and even Earth itself, were created only to serve us.

In the scientific view, however, this is not the way it was from the beginning. Earth existed for 4.6 billion years before even the first life-form that sketchily resembled a human being came into existence.

Then, for millions of years after the first hominids appeared, they were only animals like other animals, perhaps no more successful at coping with the environment than are chimpanzees today.

It was perhaps five hundred thousand years ago that hominids (at a time when *Homo sapiens* did not yet exist) first began to make use of fire, and it was only then that they had something no other animal had ever had or has ever gained since.

When *Homo sapiens* appeared on the scene, the quality of tools (axes, spears, bows-and-arrows) improved to the extent where human beings, working in coordination, could destroy much larger animals. The woolly mammoth, it is thought, was hounded to extinction by primitive Siberian hunters between ten and twenty thousand years ago.

Since then, there has been no question that human beings have mastered all other large forms of life. We have even, in the last century and a half, made headway against small forms of life such as insects, parasitic worms, and microscopic disease agents. There our domination is by no means complete, and the result is yet in doubt.

Furthermore, it is now questioned whether it is wise for human beings even to aspire to "dominion" in too literal a fashion and to take too seriously the implication of this verse of the Bible. Human beings have brought about the extinction of many species of plants and animals, and the rate at which species are being destroyed is far greater now than it has ever been before. Such extinctions may well upset the ecological balance of life as a whole.

Then, too, human beings have altered the face of the Earth in many ways by cutting down forests, planting grainfields, building dams and cities, polluting land, sea, and air with the products and wastes of their activities. This has all been done without much worry as to how these alterations are affecting the welfare of life and of human beings in particular. We may well be laying the groundwork for our own destruction.

It is becoming rather obvious that human beings would be better off to exercise their "dominion" by deciding to have less absolute "dominion." People had better think of themselves as caretakers of Earth and not as its masters.

---

27 *So God created man in his own image, in the image of God created he him; male and female* [54] *created he them.*

---

54. It would seem from this verse that both sexes were created simultaneously, and this certainly agrees with the scientific view.

In the scientific view, human beings evolved as a two-sexed animal. This had to be, since human beings were evolved from two-sexed predecessors who were in turn evolved from two-sexed predecessors all the way back to some primitive wormlike organism.

---

28 *And God blessed them, and God said unto them, Be fruitful, and multiply, and replenish the earth, and subdue it: and have dominion over the fish of the sea, and over the fowl of the air, and over every living thing that moveth upon the earth.*

29 *And God said, Behold, I have given you every herb bearing seed, which is upon the face of all the earth, and every tree, in the which is the fruit of a tree yielding seed; to you it shall be for meat.* [55]

---

55. It would appear from this verse that humanity was created with a purely vegetarian diet. ("Meat" is used

here, by the way, to mean food generally, rather than animal muscle specifically, and the Revised Standard Version uses the word "food" here.)

This is surely not so in the scientific account of man's beginning. The primates were evolved from insectivorous creatures, and many primates eat insects as well as plants. Though the gorilla is entirely vegetarian, the chimpanzee will on occasion eat meat if it has the chance.

Human beings are more nearly carnivorous than are any other primates, and hominids as far back as we can make out ate animal life when they could get it.

Undoubtedly there are human beings who are vegetarians out of a dislike for animal food, or out of humane feeling for animals, or out of some religious teaching, but I suspect that most human beings, if they consulted their own tastes, and if meat were freely available, would be carnivorous, and that this would always have been true as long as the species has existed.

---

30 *And to every beast of the earth, and to every fowl of the air, and to every thing that creepeth upon the earth, wherein there is life, I have given every green herb for meat:* [56] *and it was so.*

---

56. Apparently all animal life was created with a vegetarian diet, according to the P-document, but this is surely even less likely than it is in the case of human beings specifically. As best we can tell from our study of evolution, as soon as animals evolved, some must have eaten others.

As long as one thinks that plants are not alive in the same sense that animals are, then it is rather natural to think that plants serve the specific and sole purpose of being food for animals. From that standpoint, for one animal to eat another, for life to eat life, would seem a sort of perversion.

Once it is recognized that plants and animals are

equally alive and that all animal life eats life, then it becomes not very important whether the life eaten is plant or animal.

In fact, it is essential that animals be eaten if the components of their tissues are to be "recycled" and brought back into the general pool of material on which all living things depend for growth and multiplication. If animals were not eaten, all of potential life substance would be eventually tied up in the form of dead animals.

Of course, in default of all·else, such dead animals decay, but by decay we merely mean that they are eaten by microorganisms of which the Biblical writers were unaware. In short, a pure vegetarian diet for all animals is simply impossible.

---

31 *And God saw every thing that he had made, and, behold, it was very good. And the evening and the morning were the sixth day.*[57]

---

57. The Creation as described in the P-document took six days. Why six?

One suggestion sometimes made is that six is a "perfect number"; that is, it is the sum of all the numbers that go into it evenly ("factors") excluding itself. Those factors of 6 that are less than itself are 1, 2, and 3, and the sum is 6.

There are not very many such numbers. The next higher one is 28, whose factors, 1, 2, 4, 7, and 14, add up to 28. The next two perfect numbers are 496 and 8,128. Those were all the perfect numbers known to the ancients. Only in modern times have additional larger perfect numbers been discovered.

The concept of perfect numbers is, however, of Greek origin, and undoubtedly did not influence the writers of the P-document. There are other reasons for the six days of Creation, which I'll come back to later.

---

1 *Thus the heavens and the earth were finished, and all the host of them.*[59]

---

58. In its original form, as I said earlier, the book of Genesis was one continuous tale. The division into chapters and verses is artificial, late-made, and sometimes misleading.

For instance, the first chapter of Genesis ends with a verse that completes the sixth day; but the Creation-tale of the P-document does not end there, it goes on for three and a half more verses. It would have been far more appropriate to have allowed the first chapter to continue through those verses, but it is too late to change matters now.

59. It is not quite clear what "all the host of them" means. Can it be a reference to the angels, which some legends suppose were created before God created heaven and earth? It seems more likely that it merely refers to the infinite detail involved in the finished job—all the stars in the sky; all the geographical features on Earth; all the different plants and animals; all the interrelationship of all the items of Creation, and so on.

---

2 *And on the seventh day God ended* [60] *his work which he had made; and he rested* [61] *on the seventh day from all his work which he had made.*

---

60. We might argue about the meaning of the word "ended." In a narrow sense, it might mean that the work of God was utterly completed because it was perfect (what else would one expect of God?), and nothing further remained to be done through all eternity.

As far as human history is concerned, however, this

cannot be right, for the entire story of the Bible is that of the interplay between God and humanity. Human history, in the Biblical sense, involves the intervention of God at every stage, and details his rewards and punishments. Furthermore, God finds it in the highest degree difficult (it would seem from the Biblical account) to persuade a few human beings to maintain even a minimally acceptable code of behavior.

Suppose we suppose that human history is not included among the work that had been "ended" and confine that verb to the nonhuman background against which the human drama is played out.

Even in this narrower sense, "ended" cannot be taken literally. On Earth, we can see that the environmental background is not pristine, perfect, and unchangeable. There are alterations in the body of Earth itself. Rivers change their course, coastlines are eaten away, landslides change the configuration of mountains, and so on.

The Greek philosophers admitted that all things earthly were changeable and corrupt, but it was common for them to maintain that outside Earth's sphere, up in the skies, the heavenly machinery and the heavenly bodies themselves were unchangeable, incorruptible, and perfect. This fits in with the Judeo-Christian view that the heavenly bodies, being made for humanity, would retain all their properties unchanged until the drama of human history was done, at which time the Universe would be discarded and a new one begun on different principles. This view is given in fullest detail in Revelation, the final book of the New Testament.

In the scientific view, however, *all* is inevitable change, and the work of creation has never ended and may never end.

Since the Earth was created, biological evolution has brought into being and has ended very many species. Perhaps twenty million species (nine-tenths of all those that ever existed) have become extinct.

Nor has biological evolution stopped now. Given enough time, life forms will change markedly in appearance, structure, and function. That includes the human species. What's more, many species have become extinct in recent centuries (mostly through human agency), and many more seem to be on the point of becoming extinct. Nor is it at all beyond the bounds of possibility that the human species may become extinct someday while other life continues to go on.

The Earth itself has never stopped changing. There are not only the changes we are aware of, but changes that are so slow as to be insensible to ordinary observation over the full length of historic times. There are changes that involve the coming and going of glaciers, for instance, and the even slower shifting of the crustal plates that make up Earth's surface—which brings about the formation and creation of mountain chains, the growth of volcanoes and islands, the joining and splitting of continents.

The stars themselves (including the sun) undergo evolutionary changes of their own. All stars are mortal, as are all human beings. Stars shine at the expense of nuclear changes at their cores, and eventually those nuclear changes will run their course and each star will first expand and then collapse into a small dense body. On a few occasions, the collapse is preceded by a gigantic explosion.

How long a star will maintain itself in its "normal" state (the state in which the sun is now—called "main sequence") depends on its mass. The more massive it is the shorter lived. Some very massive stars will remain on the main sequence only a million years or so. Some small, barely red-hot stars may continue to be superficially unchanged for hundreds of billions of years.

Our sun, intermediate in size, will remain on the main sequence for perhaps as long as twelve billion years. Since five billion years have already passed, there are only seven billion years, at most, before the sun begins its expansion and Earth warms to the point where it cannot support life.

Uncounted trillions of stars must have been formed in the immediate aftermath of the big bang, and many of those stars, of moderate size, still exist. Many others have expended their main sequence life cycle, have blown away part of their substance explosively, and now live on in shrunken form; some are no larger than a few miles across.

Yet, ever since the big bang, there have also always remained in the Universe vast clouds of dust and gas out of which new stars might form. To these clouds was added the material of the exploded stars. Whereas the clouds as they formed after the big bang were made up only of hydrogen and helium, the two simplest atoms, the material added by the exploded remnants of dying stars added more complicated atoms (carbon, nitrogen, oxygen, sulfur, silicon, iron, and many others), which had been formed in the glowing core of the stars before they had exploded.

Stars that form out of dust clouds that have been contaminated with these complicated atoms are "second-generation stars." Our sun, formed nearly five billion years ago and ten billion years *after* the big bang, is such a second-generation star. The complicated atoms that are essential portions of our bodies and of all living tissues were formed out of the exploded bodies of stars dead and gone before our sun or Earth saw existence.

Nor has the creation of stars ceased after the formation of our sun. There must be stars that are younger than the sun. All the stars that are considerably brighter and larger than the sun are certainly younger than the sun, for if they and the sun were formed at the same time (such is the short lifetime of a large star), they would be exploded and dead by now. Indeed, we can observe unmistakable indications of stars being formed in clouds of dust and gas, such as the Orion Nebula, *right now*.

Whole galaxies evolve and change, and the entire Universe is evolving and changing. What the end will be, or whether there will be a true end, we cannot say, but clearly the work of creation, even allowing that it began at the big bang, has never ended but has progressed continually and is progressing right now, by all the scientific evidence we have.

61. To say that God "rested" is curiously anthropomorphic; that is, it interprets God's deeds or motives by human standards. It might seem reasonable to maintain

that God does not require rest as a human being does. Since he is perfect and omnipotent, nothing can weary him. Why, then, does the P-document describe him as resting?

For one thing, the writers of the P-document here, as elsewhere, labor to etherealize the much more anthropomorphic account of the Babylonian Creation-myth. In this myth, the numerous gods, having created the Universe, celebrate by throwing a party and having a grand time. The writers of the P-document have the one and only God do no more than gravely "rest," which can mean merely "to desist from further acts of creation."

But then, why not say "desist from creating" rather than "rest," with the latter's inevitable connotation of recovering from weariness?

One explanation is that it is impossible to describe the actions and motivation of an infinite God except by using human terms. Even though these terms fall infinitely short of a true explanation, they remain the only way of getting across any understanding at all to human minds.

Or it may be that the writers of the P-document, while improving on the Babylonian Creation-myth, had not yet reached a full understanding of the transcendence of God and labored under the sneaking suspicion that even for his superhuman nature, the work of creating the entire Universe in only six days would have induced something akin to weariness.

Indeed, through much of history, it was rather taken for granted that all motion—and all action generally—was wearisome and that even inanimate objects would stop whatever they were doing and "rest" if given a chance to do so.

This thought is natural enough since on Earth we see that moving things generally stop moving after a time; that things that rise in the air fall back; that all living things fail to maintain action indefinitely.

What causes life forms (including the human being) to grow weary is the fact that living tissue is maintained at a relatively low entropy, that living tissue is constantly changing in the direction of higher entropy, and that this

71

change must be continually neutralized and made up for and restored if life is to continue. It is the constant effort to maintain a low-entropy state that gives rise to the sensation we think of as weariness. When action causes us to fall behind in the task of maintenance, weariness increases, and when we rest, we give our body a chance to catch up on its maintenance requirements so that weariness disappears. (In the end, of course, we lose out in the struggle against the tendency for entropy to increase, and we die.)

Inanimate objects on Earth tend to stop moving because of the action of such factors as air resistance and friction. These involve an entropy increase that inanimate objects are incapable of reversing, and so their action wanes and finally "dies."

Where entropy is not a factor, however, weariness does not arise and action does not stop. Some subatomic particles, left to themselves (the proton, the electron, the photon, the neutrino, and so on), move and exist eternally and never grow weary. Certain combinations of these particles can form stable atoms, which in turn can form stable atom-combinations or molecules, which, left to themselves, are eternal.

Again, Earth and the other planets, left to themselves, will circle the sun indefinitely (in past times, it was thought that angels had to push a planet continually or it would come to a halt), and the sun will circle the Galactic center indefinitely.

All changes that take place in the inanimate portions of the Universe in the course of its creation and evolution, move, as far as we can tell, in the direction of increasing entropy. Such changes cannot induce weariness. The Universe cannot become weary of increasing entropy any more than water can grow weary of pouring downhill.

---

3 *And God blessed the seventh day, and sanctified it:* [62] *because that in it he had rested from all his work which God created and made.*

---

62. The sanctified seventh day is the "Sabbath," the day that on our calendars today is known (in English) as Saturday.

In other words, on the first Sunday, God created light; on Monday, he created the sky; on Tuesday, he created the dry land and its cover of vegetation; on Wednesday, he created the heavenly bodies; on Thursday, he created the animal life of the sea and air; on Friday, he created the animal life of the land and then created human beings; and finally, on Saturday, he rested.

Although the P-document would make it appear that the Sabbath was divinely instituted at the time of creation and before human history began, it would seem that in the period before the Babylonian exile—in the time of the Judges and Kings of Israel—the Sabbath was little regarded.

It was only during and after the Babylonian activity that the Sabbath became all-important and was written into not only the Creation-tale but into the Ten Commandments as well. What was the connection between the Sabbath and the Babylonians?

The word "sabbath" is from a Hebrew word meaning "to break off" or "to stop," and it seems to be connected with a period when one ceases from one's daily labors.

It is necessary to interrupt work by rest and sleep, and more is accomplished in the long run by an individual who takes time off to rest and sleep than by someone who tries to work continuously. In the same way, it may be argued that occasionally there should be a longer rest and sleep—a whole day off, in other words—and that this, too, would lead to more being accomplished in the long run.

But when does the day off come? At regular intervals or at irregular ones? If regular, then after how many workdays does the rest day come?

In those primitive times in history, when human beings lived in family groups and no more, days off undoubtedly came whenever the state of things permitted or the family leader felt like permitting them. As society grew more complex, such days off had to be regulated if the work of the community was not to lose in efficiency. The best way of doing that was to tie it to religion.

The people of the Tigris-Euphrates had developed a lunar calendar probably before 2000 B.C. The appearance of each new moon, signifying the start of a new month, was the occasion of a religious festival, and eventually other phases of the moon were celebrated.

It was the full moon that was first called "sabbath" (*sabbatu* to the Akkadians, who dominated the Tigris-Euphrates valley in the third millennium B.C.). This notion spread out to neighboring lands, and in Israel, before the Babylonian captivity, the full moon (sabbath) and new moon may have been treated as equally important.

Thus, when a woman plans to go to the wonder-working prophet Elisha to persuade him to revive her dead son, her husband says, ". . . Wherefore wilt thou go to him today? It is neither new moon, nor sabbath . . ." (2 Kings 4:23).

By the time of the Babylonian captivity, however, the Babylonians were also celebrating the intermediate phases of the moon; the first-quarter, when the moon is a semicircle on its way from new to full, and the third-quarter, when the moon is a semicircle on its way back from full to new.

These four phases come at intervals of about a week, and the very word "week" (*Woche* in German) is derived from an old Teutonic word meaning "change" (*Wechsel* in German)—that is, the change of the moon's phase.

Each phase comes at an interval of not quite 7.4 days, so that in order to keep the week in time with the lunar months, the week should be sometimes seven days long and sometimes eight in some set pattern. This was not done. The Babylonians chose to make the week an unvarying seven days long, even though this meant that the week lost all connection with the lunar month.

The probable reason for this was that there happened to be seven "planets" in the sky that changed position regularly against the background of the fixed stars: the sun, the moon, Mercury, Venus, Mars, Jupiter, and Saturn.

To the Babylonians, it seemed to make astrological sense to suppose that each planet was in charge of a particular day (since each planet was in turn the province of a particular god). An eighth day in a week would be a day without a planet-god in charge, and this was unthinkable. The seven-day week it was, therefore, and one day in the week was given over to a religious celebration, and work was suspended either to allow time for the celebration or because the day was considered unlucky.

The Jews in Babylonian exile naturally observed the weekly day of rest, but could not accept the polytheistic religious justification and had to evolve one of their own.

The writers of the P-document therefore grounded it in the week of creation—six days of divine labor and one day of divine rest. It was a case of the labors of God himself being made to fit the Babylonian week. That is why Creation took six days rather than any other number of days, and it is an explanation that does not involve the Greek concept of perfect numbers.

Coming back from Babylonian exile, the Jews instituted an all-important Sabbath festival, and this was carried over into Christian ways of thought. Christians, however, abandoned the seventh day, little by little, and placed increasing emphasis on "the Lord's Day" (Sunday), which was the day of the week on which Jesus had been reported to have undergone the Resurrection. The Moslems celebrate Friday.

The week is now part of the general calendar used the world over.

From the scientific standpoint, the week is a purely artificial division that unnecessarily complicates the calendar. There are fifty-two weeks and one day in ordinary years and fifty-two weeks and two days in leap years. These additional days mean that every year starts on a different day of the week from the year before in a complex twenty-eight-year cycle.

If those extra days were celebrated as additional days of rest without any weekday assigned to them, the calendar could be made to repeat itself exactly, year after year. Indeed, it could easily be arranged to have every three-month interval repeat itself exactly over and over.

To set up so convenient and sensible a calendar seems, however, to be completely impossible because of the unwillingness of most people—Jews, Christians, and Moslems alike—to allow any modification whatever in the concept of the week.

Thus, the accident of the existence of seven visible planets; the fact that the Babylonians tied these in, astrologically, with the days of the week; the further fact that the writers of the P-document kept the Babylonian week but sanitized it and tied it in with the tale of Creation—make it inevitable that we continue to use an unnecessarily clumsy and inconvenient calendar despite the fact that it could so easily be patched up.

---

4 *These are the generations of the heavens and of the earth when they were created,[63] in the day [64] that the Lord God [65] made the earth and the heavens,*

---

63. This phrase ends the P-document Creation-tale with a final summarizing sentence that can be paraphrased into modern language as "These are the stages by which the heavens and earth were created."

64. Here the artificial division of the books of the Bible into verses creates an infelicity, for this verse places in a single sentence the ending of one Creation-tale and the beginning of another, with only a comma to separate the two.

In the Revised Standard Version, a period replaces the comma, and the second part of the verse begins a new paragraph, thus:

"These are the generations of the heavens and the earth when they were created.

"In the day that the Lord God made the earth and the heavens,"—notice that the verse ends in a comma; the second sentence is incomplete and is continued in the next verse.

It seems reasonable to ask how we know that we have here a second Creation-tale. The traditional view, after all, is that the entire Bible is divinely inspired by God, word for word, and that it can therefore contain no errors and certainly no internal contradictions (except those introduced by faulty copying or erroneous translation).

From that standpoint, this second tale is supposed to supplement the first one and be in accord with it; therefore it is not really a second tale at all, merely a more detailed version of the first one concentrating on the creation of humanity.

The second Creation-tale is so different from the first in so many of its details, and has a so-distinctly more primitive atmosphere, that to make it fit the first one requires tortuous reasoning and argument. It is much simpler and more straightforward (if one can bear to abandon the theory of divine inspiration) to recognize that we have one Creation-tale based on the best science of the day and a second one that is a folktale derived from relatively unsophisticated sources.

Probably, the second tale was the one current in at least parts of Israel well before the Babylonian exile, and it was so well known that it simply could not be left out of the Bible. Therefore, the editors who put the Bible into its present form, while putting the P-document Creation-tale first, also put in the earlier, more primitive tale second and relied on ingenious interpretation to explain away any contradictions.

65. The clearest indication of the switch from one tale to another is the reference to "Lord God" in this verse; in the first 34 verses of the Bible, the reference has been only to "God."

The Hebrew word translated here as "Lord" consists of four letters, which transliterated into the nearest English equivalents would be YHVH. Rationalist interpretation of the Bible was first advanced by German scholars, however, so that the four letters are frequently seen as JHWH, since the German J and W are pronounced like the English Y and V. YHVH, or JHWH, is referred to as the tetragrammaton, from Greek words meaning four letters.

The tetragrammaton represents the personal name of God, and the mere fact that it is used in this verse, whereas earlier it was not used, is an indication that we are now dealing with a second writer or a second source. (Reasons have been advanced for the change in an attempt to avoid assuming a second document—such as saying that "God" represents the deity in his aspect of stern justice, and "Lord God" in his aspect of loving mercy—but such reasons sound artificial and unconvincing. It is much easier to accept the fact that the early chapters of Genesis are derived from two different sources.)

The difference in name is itself an indication that the second Creation-tale is more primitive than that described by the P-document. The assumption that the transcendent deity has a name after the fashion of human beings is very much like the assumption that he has a body shaped like ours or emotions like ours, and the P-document avoids it.

"Lord" is not the name of God, by the way, and it is not a translation of YHVH. Actually, we don't know what the translation of YHVH is exactly; that is, what it means in English. Apparently, it gets across the idea of TO BE in all its tenses. YHVH is "that which is, was, and shall be," and if that is indeed what it means or implies then one can hardly think of a better name for an eternal God.

As the Jews' concept of God grew ever more exalted and abstract, they did not wish to profane the holy name by even pronouncing it, so the custom grew of substituting a title for the name. Whenever YHVH appeared in the Biblical text or in a liturgy, the Jews would say Adonai (meaning "the Lord") instead. Therefore, YHVH Elohim became Adonai Elohim, which is translated "the Lord God."

The Hebrew language in its written form consists of consonants only. The vowels are not included, but to people who know the language, that does not matter.

As Hebrew became less familiar to the Jews, however, and as the common language of everyday use became Aramaic in Persian times, it became customary to make the vowel sounds in Hebrew by diacritical marks under the letters so that those unfamiliar with Hebrew could pronounce the words correctly. For YHVH, however, the vowels indicated were those for *Adonai,* since that was all one was supposed to say.

Using those vowels, YHVH became "Yehovah" or (later, because of German influence) "Jehovah." Either way, that is not the name of God, because the vowels are wrong.

We cannot say for sure what the name is, for there is no record of the correct vowels in the cautious writings of the Jews. (Only the high priest was supposed to pronounce the actual name of God, and that only when he was alone in the Holy of Holies within the Temple and only at the time of Yom Kippur—and there hasn't been a high priest or a Temple, in the Biblical sense of the term, for 1,900 years.)

It is thought that the name of God is *Yahveh* (which may also be spelled *Jahveh, Jahweh,* or even *Jawe*).

The second Creation-tale is therefore part of the J-document, where the J stands for the first letter of the tetragrammaton in its German version.

It also happens that the J-document consists of legends current in the southern part of the territory occupied by the tribes of Israel, the part that between 933 B.C. and 586 B.C. made up the Kingdom of Judah. The J of the J-document can therefore just as aptly stand for Judah.

---

5 *And every plant of the field before it was in the earth, and every herb of the field before it grew: for the Lord God had not caused it to rain upon the earth,*[66] *and there was not a man to till the ground.*

---

66. The language of the King James Version is not very clear here. If we were telling the tale in colloquial English, the last part of the preceding verse, together with this one, would read: "When the Lord God made the earth and the heavens there was, to begin with, no vegetation, for there was no rain, and no person had yet been created to till the ground."

In the P-document Creation-tale, which borrowed heavily from the Babylonians, water predominated first, chaotically, and on the third day, God had to push the water aside and allow the dry land to emerge. This is an appropriate assumption as to the original state of the world for the Babylonians, who are a river civilization and who have to contend with flood constantly. The dry land seems a precious asset to them, to be won with difficulty from the encroaching waters.

The J-document Creation-tale also borrowed from Babylonian legend, but less selectively and over a longer period of time, during which changes could be introduced to suit the circumstances of a different locale. The Judeans were essentially a desert people, and to them it was dry land that was natural, even excessive, while water was a precious commodity to be viewed as a gift of God.

The J-document, then, starts with a dry and barren Earth that bears no life. Nor is there any mention of light, sky, or heavenly bodies. The full focus is on Earth and humanity. This is a more limited concept of Creation than that of the P-document, but the J-document assumption of an Earth that is dry to begin with is closer to the scientific point of view than the P-document's assumption of an Earth that is wet to begin with.

---

6 *But there went up a mist from the earth, and watered the whole face of the ground.*[67]

---

67. The Hebrew word *ayd*, of which "mist" is the translation given in the King James, is a rare word that occurs in only one other place in the Bible (Job 36:27). The translation is not certain; it could be a "flow of water" or even a "flood."

It is very tempting to suppose that it refers to an uprising of water from the primordial dry ground to form the oceans and other waters of the Earth. Thus, whereas the P-document forms the dry land by separating it from the primordial muddy ocean, the J-document forms the ocean by producing it from the primordial dry land.

Here again it is the J-document, the more primitive of the two, that is closer to the scientific view of the Earth's origins—surprisingly close in this respect. As I explained earlier, the oceans and atmosphere are thought to have formed secondarily, as the solid material of the originally dry and airless Earth slowly evolved its separate layers.

---

7 *And the Lord God formed man of the dust of the ground,[68] and breathed into his nostrils the breath of life;[69] and man became a living soul.[70]*

---

68. Presumably, once there was water, it could be mixed with clay and a man could be formed just as a potter would form a pot. In fact, from the wording of this verse, one has an unavoidable picture of the Lord God actually playing the role of potter and physically shaping the figure of a man.

It is common for legends of the beginning of human beings to state them to have been formed of clay and to have been molded by a divine being. This is true of legends in Egypt, Babylonia, and Greece. In the Greek tales, the Titan, Prometheus, molded the first human beings out of clay.

However natural the assumption of man-as-a-complex-pot in a primitive age when the potter's wheel was the most delicate known technique for forming complex shapes, it is far out of line with the modern scientific view. The atoms in clay are not at all the kind that are common in living tissue. If the description had been of man being formed of coal dust and water, it would have been more impressive.

The Hebrew word for man in this verse is *adam,* and the Hebrew word for dust is *adamah.* This is not a coincidence. Primitive people do not imagine words to be simple inventions. It seems natural to them, as I said earlier in the book, to imagine that a name belongs to a thing as an integral part and that to the name is associated all the characteristics of the thing itself.

If two words are similar, it would then bespeak some sort of connection between the things. It is as though one were to wonder why a large rope is called a "hawser" and then decide it is because one would have to be as strong as a horse to break it. This sort of thing is called word-play when it is meant in fun, folk etymology if it is meant seriously. The early books of the Bible are full of folk etymology.

If the words *adam* and *adamah* had just happened to be similar, it would have been taken as good evidence that man was originally made of dust. It might also be that *adam* arose from *adamah* after the legend was established, replacing an older word for man—or the other way around to replace an older word for dust.

Notice that in the P-document Creation-tale, man is formed last of all living things and by the word of God alone, as nearly as we can tell. This creation is the climactic act, and man is brought into a Universe that has been prepared for him to the last detail.

In the J-document, on the other hand, man is formed first of all living things. God physically shapes him as a potter would, bringing him forth into a barren world and then arranging a suitable environment for him. This is a much more primitive concept.

69. Even with God himself as potter, the clay figure that results, however marvelous in appearance, is quite as dead as the original lump. To make it more than clay requires the divine magic of life. This constitutes the breath that, as I explained earlier, represents the Spirit of God. In other words, a nonliving shaped object of matter was infused with a bit of the Spirit of God and became alive.

From the modern scientific view, however, we know that the breath is as material as the rest of the body and will not suffice to represent the immaterial essence of either life or God. In fact, there is no material thing that is the essence of life, but rather the complexity of organization that brings it into being. Life is a biochemical-biophysical process, rather than a thing.

To have the verse approach scientific language more closely, one might paraphrase it something as follows: "And the Lord God formed man out of clay and then imposed upon the clay the complexity of organization characteristic of life."

70. "Soul" is the translation of the Hebrew *nephesh,* and it is very difficult to tell what it means. The chances are that the best translation would be "and man became a living being."

Nowadays, a common view of the soul is that it is some sort of spiritual essence, utterly immaterial, that is inserted into a person at birth (or at conception) and that departs from a person at death; that it is an immortal component of man that is neither born nor dies but is housed in the body for the brief period of that body's existence on Earth. All this is actually derived from Greek thought, and in that sense, "soul" is a translation of the Greek *psyche* and not of the Hebrew *nephesh.*

From the scientific viewpoint, there is no evidence in favor of the existence of a soul or of any immaterial essence that departs at death. What happens at death is that the complex organization of the living organism breaks down to the point where what remains is insufficient to maintain the complex of chemical and physical changes we call life.

In recent years, there have been reports of people who were "clinically dead" and who, upon revival, tell stories that sound as though they have experienced an afterlife. These are subjective reports elicited by eager questioners from very sick people; as far as I know, no reputable biologist takes the reports seriously.

---

8 *And the Lord God planted a garden* [71] *eastward in Eden;* [72] *and there he put the man whom he had formed.* [73]

---

71. According to the J-document, it is only after the man had been created that God proceeded to make the earth suitable for him to live in. Food, in the form of vegetation, was created for him.

In the P-document, the creation of vegetation was described as, "And God said, Let the earth bring forth grass—" and the word of God was sufficient.

It might be that this occurred in the J-document when the "mist . . . watered the whole face of the ground," but the J-document does not specifically say so—though I suppose it might be argued that it goes without saying. (This is a dangerous argument. If one thing goes without saying, almost anything can.)

Even if the garden here described is only a patch of land particularly suited to the needs of the man God had created in a world that was already covered with vegetation, it is interesting that God "planted" that garden.

One might again argue that God planted it with a word, nothing more, and that this, too, goes without saying. The actual use of the word "planted" without further explanation inevitably gives rise, however, to the image of God as a farmer as well as of a potter—which fits the generally primitive nature of the J-document.

72. Where was Eden, within which the Garden was located? There have been incredible quantities of speculation about this, some of it pretty wild. Actually, however, there may be no mystery about it at all.

In the first place, it was "eastward"; eastward, that is, from the place where the tale was told; eastward from the land of Israel, in other words.

To the east of Israel is the Tigris-Euphrates valley. The first civilization to exist in the lower reaches of this valley was that of the Sumerians, and in the Sumerian language, the word eden means "plain."

No one knows where, exactly, the Sumerians came from, but if, as seems likely, they originally entered the area from the hilly regions to the northeast, they may well have thought of themselves as coming to Eden; that is, to the "plain."

Furthermore, the hilly regions may well have been

areas where it was hard to find food, while in the plain along the lower Tigris and Euphrates, there was marvelous farmland. With the proper irrigation from the waters of the rivers, the harvests were plentiful, the land bountiful, the living good. To the Sumerians it was like coming to a garden in the plain—a "garden in Eden."

Things may not have stayed wonderful for long. As population increased, food became harder to get. Warfare came as the Sumerian city-states squabbled with each other. There may well have grown a longing for the earliest days in Sumeria, when the land was really a "garden of Eden," until the phrase came to symbolize a golden age of the past, which may have only been vaguely identified with the actual region in which the Sumerians continued to live and which was no longer in a golden age.

In Hebrew, eden means "delight" or "enjoyment," but this is merely an accidental similarity of sound with the Sumerian eden, for the two languages are not related. (In fact, Sumerian is not related to any known language.) Nevertheless, the accidental Hebrew meaning helped crystallize the feeling that Eden might be a mystical term without actual geographic meaning and that the place originally inhabited by mankind was merely "the garden of delight," with no place name at all.

It seems pretty reasonable, however, to suppose that what the verse is really saying is that "the Lord God planted a garden eastward in Sumeria."

73. It would seem, then, by this verse, that the first man lived in Sumeria.

From the scientific view this is not so. The first creatures that can be considered hominids, it seems fairly certain, evolved in eastern Africa, in what is now the region of Kenya and Tanzania. It may have been only after hundreds of thousands of years that hominids reached the Tigris-Euphrates valley. (On the other hand, we don't know yet where the first creatures that might be considered Homo sapiens originated.)

Suppose, though, we consider "civilized man." The earliest civilization sufficiently advanced to include writing was the Sumerian. There, writing came into use as early, perhaps, as 3500 B.C. All other early civilizations developed writing after the Sumerians did, and that includes the Egyptians and the Chinese. The Sumerians were first in the field with mathematics and astronomy, too.

Therefore, if we think of the man God created not as the first man, but as the first civilized man, putting him in Sumeria rather matches the historical facts.

---

9 *And out of the ground made the Lord God to grow every tree that is pleasant to the sight, and good for food;* [74] *the tree of life* [75] *also in the midst of the garden, and the tree of knowledge of good and evil.* [76]

---

74. Apparently the Garden was intended to contain everything that man could want and need, and in later times, it was looked upon as an idyllic place of perfection, a "paradise" (which is a Greek word, of Persian origin, meaning "park" or "garden").

It is very common in legends to speak of an early "golden age," when care was absent and food was so plentiful it could be picked off the trees without labor. Why not? Each human being in reasonable circumstances can recall a golden age of his own—when he was young. Even if it was not really a golden age, it is recalled as one in older years, when the good is remembered with advantage and the bad diminishes into quaintness.

Societies usually think back upon a golden age, too. I have talked earlier of Sumerian society growing less satisfactory as population increased and internecine warfare arose. Then, too, the land was invaded about 2500 B.C. by the Akkadians, who founded an empire within which the Sumerians were a subject people. Would not the Sumerians *then* look back with nostalgia and wishfulness at a time when they were free, a golden age of great days "in Eden" ("on the plain")?

For many centuries, there would be legends of a Garden of Eden, a paradise in Sumeria when all was well and wonderful, and it would be picked up and carried on, long after the Sumerians who first told it were gone, their culture had died off and vanished, and their language had been forgotten—until it reached the Israelites at last, who retold it in their own fashion and spread it to all the world.

75. The tree of life, it is to be assumed, is a tree bearing fruit that can convey immortality when eaten—a primitive concept that is common in ancient myths.

Human beings find it difficult to live with the fact of mortality. We are, as far as we know, the only living species that is aware of the inevitability of death; the inevitability not only of death in general, but of our own personal death. (It may be that our beliefs in an immortal soul and in a life hereafter are ways of circumventing the unacceptable fact of an inevitable death.)

Yet, in human myths, the gods are almost always immortal. Perhaps there is a trick to it; something the gods know that they won't tell to mortal men. Many cultures have legends in which some hero searches for the secret of immortality—though he never succeeds for, alas, we are still mortal.

The ancient Sumerians had a tale of Gilgamesh, king of Erech (one of the Sumerian city-states), who was in search of eternal life. It is the oldest epic of which we have knowledge and was, in its time, undoubtedly very popular. The tale of Gilgamesh may have influenced the Greek legends of Hercules, and the tree of life in the Garden of Eden may itself be there under the influence of Gilgamesh's quest.

76. The tree of knowledge of good and evil, it is to be assumed, is a tree bearing fruit that can convey knowledge when eaten. It is usually supposed that the particular type of knowledge it controlled was that of moral awareness, of being able to distinguish between good and evil. However, "good and evil" is a Hebrew idiom meaning everything (since every thing is either good or evil; to know both is to know everything), so that the fruit of the tree conveys knowledge generally.

10 *And a river went out of Eden to water the garden;* [77] *and from thence it was parted,* [78] *and became into four heads.* [79]

---

77. The oldest civilizations of humanity grew up around rivers; certainly, the Sumerian civilization did. It is therefore reasonable to have a river watering the Garden.

The river "went out of Eden," but that doesn't mean it originated in the Garden and flowed out of it. Eden is not the Garden itself (people often confused the two), but merely the land in which the Garden was located.

If we assume that the Garden was in the lower reaches of the Tigris-Euphrates valley, we might assume that it was either the Tigris or the Euphrates river, and we might ask which.

The Tigris and Euphrates flow southeastward from their sources in what is now eastern Turkey, in a roughly parallel path. At one point, about 350 miles from the Persian Gulf, they approach within twenty-five miles of each other, then move apart before approaching again.

In the time of the Sumerians, the Euphrates and the Tigris entered the Persian Gulf by separate mouths about a hundred miles apart.

At that time, however, the Persian Gulf extended about 175 miles farther to the northwest than it now does. The rivers, however, carried mud and silt with them and slowly formed a delta that filled in the upper end of the narrow Persian Gulf.

The Tigris and the Euphrates continued to flow over the new land as it formed, the Tigris flowing south and the Euphrates east. Eventually, they met to form a single joined river, the Shatt-al-Arab, which is now 120 miles long.

The Shatt-al-Arab was already in existence by the time the Jews were in Babylonian captivity, after which the Book of Genesis was put into its present form.

It may be that the Biblical writers considered the Shatt-al-Arab to be the river flowing out of Eden (Sumeria) into the Garden and from thence into the Persian

Gulf. The Garden may have been viewed as existing just downstream from the point where the Tigris and Euphrates rivers flowed into each other.

This delta land did not yet exist in Sumerian times, but the Biblical writers may not have known that.

78. The phrase "and from thence it was parted" sounds as though it means that after the river flowed out of the garden, it divided. We take it for granted that in describing what happens to a river, we move (in imagination) in the direction the water is flowing. That is a reasonable convention, but it is not a cosmic law.

Suppose that from our vantage point in the Garden on the upper reaches of the Shatt-al-Arab, we look upstream. We would see that the river does part and become two large rivers, the Euphrates and the Tigris.

79. The verse says that the river parts into "four heads" (that is, four rivers), and the Tigris and Euphrates are only two. Nevertheless, both rivers have their tributaries. These tributaries may be rivers or large man-made canals, since from Sumerian times onward, through all of Biblical history, the Babylonian region was crisscrossed by irrigation canals.

---

11 *The name of the first is Pison:* [80] *that is it which compasseth the whole land of Havilah,* [81] *where there is gold;* [82]

---

80. Pison (or Pishon) cannot be identified with any river known today. Nor is it mentioned elsewhere in the Bible.

81. Havilah, like Pison, cannot be identified with any region known today. Unlike Pison, however, it is mentioned elsewhere in the Bible, notably in a passage where there is described the region in which the Ishmaelite tribes lived: "And they dwelt from Havilah unto Shur . . ." (Genesis 25:18).

It is reasonably certain that the Ishmaelites were tribes

of the north-Arabian borderland between Judea and Babylonia. Without trying to pin it down too carefully, we can suppose that Havilah was somewhere south and west of the Euphrates River.

The Pison may therefore have been a tributary of the Euphrates, flowing into it from the west at a point above the junction of the Euphrates with the Tigris. It may not have been an important stream to begin with, and in the gradual desiccation of the area in historic times, it may have disappeared.

In fact, it may have been gone even in Biblical times, but the Biblical writer, putting the story into its final form, may have had available to him reference to older Sumerian writings (already two thousand years in *his* past) that referred to it.

82. The reference to gold has served as a red herring. In earlier times, when "the Indies" were thought to be the very epitome of wealth, it was impossible to think of gold without thinking of India. Consequently, there were suggestions that Havilah was India and the Pison River was the Indus.

That, however, is unlikely in the highest degree. The Indus River nowhere in its course comes closer than twelve hundred miles to the Tigris-Euphrates valley. Besides, India is mentioned in the Bible, in the Book of Esther, and its name in Hebrew is *Hoddu* (note the similarity to Hindu), not Havilah.

---

12 *And the gold of that land is good: there is bdellium* [83] *and the onyx stone.*

---

83. "Bdellium" is a direct Latinization of the Hebrew word *bedholah*. We don't know what bedholah is, but the usual guess is that it is some sort of aromatic gum.

The only other mention of bdellium in the Bible occurs during the period when the Israelites were wandering in the desert and feeding on manna. Concerning the manna, the Bible says, ". . . and the colour thereof as the colour of bdellium" (Numbers 11:7). Since we don't know the color of manna, that doesn't help us identify bdellium.

---

13 And the name of the second river is Gihon: [84] the same is it that compasseth the whole land of Ethiopia.[85]

---

84. Gihon, like Pison, is completely unknown, and is mentioned nowhere else in the Bible.

85. Ethiopia is what the King James Bible calls the nation whose name in this verse is, in Hebrew, *Kush*. In the Revised Standard Version, the word is not translated and is given as Cush.

There are indeed places in the Bible where Kush seems to stand for a region called Ethiopia by the Greeks. The Greek Ethiopia is not the modern nation of Abyssinia in east-central Africa, which is the familiar Ethiopia of today. Instead, the Greek Ethiopia is the region along the Nile directly south of Egypt. This was called Nubia in ancient times and now makes up the northern portion of the nation of Sudan.

If Kush really represented Nubia, then the Gihon would have to be the Nile River, which certainly "compasseth," or winds through (an alternate translation of the Hebrew word), that land.

The Nile River can't be what is meant, however, because that never approaches closer than 900 miles to the Tigris-Euphrates. The Jews of Biblical times knew that, because they knew the Nile very well.

One might argue that in ancient times, the source of the Tigris and Euphrates might not have been known very well to people acquainted only with the lower courses of the river and that the sources of the Indus and the Nile were not known at all. The Jews of Babylonian times might have imagined that all four rivers had their source from the same spring somewhere in Armenia and that, about that common spring, there was located the Garden of Eden.

That, however, is a relatively modern piece of imagining. There is no indication anywhere in ancient Jewish literature that this was believed.

Yet, if the Gihon is not the Nile, what river is it, and where is it located? The answer may lie in an alternate interpretation of Kush, one that does not involve Ethiopia/Nubia.

More often than not, the Biblical Kush refers to some desert tribe, and there is a reasonable possibility that it refers to the land of the people whom the ancient Greek geographers spoke of as the Kosseans, and whom modern historians refer to as the Kassites. They dwelt east of the Tigris and had a period of greatness between 1600 and 1200 B.C., when they invaded, conquered, and controlled the Tigris-Euphrates valley.

The Gihon, then, winding through the land of the Kassites, might represent a tributary of the Tigris, joining it from the east before the Tigris joins the Euphrates. Like the Pison, it may now be gone.

---

14 *And the name of the third river is Hiddekel:* [86] *that is it which goeth toward the east of Assyria.* [87] *And the fourth river is Euphrates.* [88]

---

86. Hiddekel is the Hebrew version of the Assyrian *i-di-ik-lat.* Unlike the quieter Euphrates, the Hiddekel is not a navigable river. It is perhaps because of the savage danger of its turbulence that the Greeks gave it the name *Tigris* ("tiger"), the name by which we know it today.

87. The description of the Hiddekel (Tigris) as going toward the east of Assyria is incorrect as it stands, for Assyria controlled land on both sides of the river throughout its history. However, the word "Assyria" is a translation of the Hebrew *Asshur,* which is the name not only of the nation, but of its first capital city. The city of

Asshur was indeed founded on the western banks of the Tigris, so that the river flows to the east of the city.

88. The Euphrates (*Perat* in Hebrew) is merely mentioned. It is entirely too well known to the Jews to require any detail.

If we imagine, then, the Garden to have been along the upper reaches of the Shatt-al-Arab, and if we look upstream, we see that the river divides into the Euphrates and the Tigris, that the Euphrates then divides into the main stream and (possibly) the tributary Pison, while the Tigris divides into the main stream and (possibly) the tributary Gihon. Looking from west to east (or left to right) we would have Pison, Euphrates, Tigris, and Gihon.

---

15 *And the Lord God took the man, and put him into the garden of Eden to dress it and to keep it.*[89]

---

89. "To dress it and to keep it" means to cultivate the Garden, something which, as any gardener or orchard-keeper would testify, requires considerable care and labor. However, the feeling one gets is that the Garden of Eden was easier to care for than a garden of today would be; that it was an ideal garden that virtually cared for itself.

The man therefore would be a food-gatherer, eating the products of trees and other plants which would be available in never-ending profusion.

As a picture of the beginning of human history, this fits in with the facts in a way. *Homo sapiens* was a food-gatherer for most of his existence on Earth, although he gathered animal food as well, when he could.

---

16 *And the Lord God commanded the man, saying, of every tree of the garden thou mayest freely eat:*

17 *But of the tree of the knowledge of good and evil, thou shalt not eat of it:* [90] *for in the day that thou eatest thereof thou shalt surely die.* [91]

---

90. This setting up of a forbidden action is common in folklore and is an easy way of explaining the presence of evil. If people are reluctant to suppose that evil can be visited upon them by an all-powerful divine being who is viewed as ultimately good, one can suppose that evil is a punishment brought by human beings upon themselves as a consequence of their own thoughtless, foolish, sinful, or vicious actions.

In the Greek myths, at the very start of human history, Pandora is given a box by the gods and is warned not to open it. She does, and all the ills of humanity escape at once

The phrase "this is the one thing you mustn't do" in any legend or folktale is invariably followed by that being the one thing the person warned must and does do. A well-known example in modern children's tales is that of Bluebeard, who warns his wife that although she may freely go into every room in his castle during his absence, she must not enter one room. He even shows her the key to the room and gives it to her, but tells her it is a key she must not use. It probably surprises not a single child when it turns out that Bluebeard's wife can barely wait for him to get out of sight before she uses the key.

In the P-document, incidentally, God gives the entire vegetable world to the animal world as food. He makes no exceptions and sets up no warnings.

91. As it reads, the verse sounds as though the fruit of the tree of knowledge is a deadly poison and will kill the man if he eats it.

This does not turn out to be the case, but one can interpret the phrase in a less literal sense. Eating the fruit may kill the man spiritually, destroying his innocence and filling him with sin. Or else eating the fruit may simply make him mortal. He may not be dead at the moment of eating, but he will know from that moment that it will be inevitable that someday he will die.

The implication is that if the man were to refrain from eating the fruit, he would never die but would be immortal. This, of course, has no basis in fact as far as the scientific study of the history of humanity is concerned. There was never a time when human beings were immortal or when any multicellular creature was.

Nevertheless, the dream of immortality has always been with human beings throughout history, and there are inevitable legends of having immortality in the palm of one's hands briefly—and then losing it.

Thus, in the well-known epic, Gilgamesh searches for immortality and manages to gain a branch of a plant that grows at the bottom of the ocean, a branch with the power of restoring youth. (It is this that may have inspired the "tree of life," which also grows in the Garden.)

But then Gilgamesh falls asleep, and while he is sleeping, the branch of immortality is stolen by a serpent.

Why by a serpent? In the first place, serpents creep through the underbrush and easily go unnoticed so that they make excellent and efficient sneak thieves. Secondly, serpents shed their skins, the outermost dead layer of it, doing so all in a piece instead of (as we do) tiny flake by tiny flake in an unnoticeable dandruff. The new layer of serpent-skin underneath the cast-off layer is bright and shiny.

Serpents live out normal lifetimes, never growing younger (any more than any other form of life does), and eventually die. To the casual observer, however, at a time when biology was but an infant study, it would seem that the snake, in shedding its skin and possessing a new gleam, had renewed its youth. It must then have some magic rejuvenating trick that human beings did not possess—because Gilgamesh had lost it to the serpent.

The test of obedience, with mortality as the threat to failure, might have been anything, by the way. Why was it the fruit of the tree of knowledge?

The feeling is all too common that knowledge is dangerous; that people are innocent and virtuous when they are unsophisticated, but that gaining knowledge introduces temptations and opportunities that lead to sin and to destruction. We all know about the innocent country lad as opposed to the evil city slicker.

And all of us, when troubled by a changing world, moan for an older and simpler time before all these "newfangled" things had ruined it all.

Thus, Thomas Grey wrote a poem in 1742 about schoolboys at play at Eton College—so happy and without the cares and worries that growing knowledge and adulthood would bring them. He says, "Where ignorance is bliss, / 'Tis folly to be wise."

The Bible says, "For in much wisdom is much grief: and he that increaseth knowledge increaseth sorrow" (Ecclesiastes 1:18).

---

18 *And the Lord God said, It is not good that the man should be alone;* [92] *I will make him an help meet for him.* [93]

---

92. In the P-document Creation-tale, human beings were created in two sexes ("male and female created he them"). In the J-document Creation-tale, a man alone is created, and not a woman. Indeed, no animals have yet been formed. The man is the only living thing in the world aside from the plant life in the Garden. At least, nothing else at all has been mentioned in the J-document.

93. The sentence "I will make him an help meet for him" suffers a bit from archaism. The Revised Standard Bible says, "I will make him a helper fit for him," and we might say in modern paraphrase, "I will make him a friend and partner."

Eventually, as the word "meet" meaning "suitable" passed out of use, the sentence came to be taken to mean "I will make him an helpmeet for him," with the single word "helpmeet" meaning "wife." The expression was corrupted further to "helpmate" (which is not a bad expression for "wife" at that).

19 *And out of the ground the Lord God formed every beast of the field, and every fowl of the air;* [94] *and brought them unto Adam* [95] *to see what he would call them:* [96] *and whatsoever Adam called every living creature, that was the name thereof.*[97]

94. It is only now in the J-document Creation-tale that the animal world generally is created, and in this respect also, it is more primitive than the P-document Creation-tale, in which the animal world is created first and man then crowns it. Certainly, the latter is a closer approach to the evolutionary view of the history of life.

Furthermore, God is again pictured (if the words of the verse are taken literally) as forming each animal out of clay (ground, dust), as a potter would.

No mention is made in the J-document Creation-tale of the formation of sea life, by the way. The J-document limits itself not only to Earth exclusively, but to the land areas of Earth.

95. This is the first place in the King James Version in which the man is called "Adam," as though that were his personal name. In Hebrew, he is referred to as *Adam* from the beginning, but that means merely "the man." The Revised Standard Version continues to refer to him as "the man" in this verse and for a number of verses following.

96. In most cultures, names tend to be confused with things. To know a name and to be able to speak it at will is to have power over it and, therefore, over the thing it represents as well. For that reason, we have to be careful how we use names, especially the names of important people who might resent the implication of being in our power.

Thus, in our own culture, while our family name is for general use, we tend to consider the first name to be reserved for friends, relations, and powerful people who *do* control us in one way or another. The most democratic of us would resent it, just a bit, if we were addressed by first name by an employee, a child, or a casual stranger of no prepossessing appearance. In some cultures, special names are kept secret; only public names that are not "true" are used, so that no one can gain power over a person.

High officials, in the role of their office, cannot be addressed by name, but only by some honorific: "Mr. President," "Your Honor," "Your Majesty," and God in particular must never be named. Even in addressing him as Lord, you must use circumspection. Any reference to God casually, or under inappropriate conditions, or as an expletive, or, worst of all, to swear falsely in his name ("to take his name in vain")—that is, for no suitable purpose—is itself a blasphemy.

Therefore, when the animals are brought to the man for names, that is a way of placing them in the man's power and in the power of mankind generally. That is a more primitive version of the passage in the P-document Creation-tale in which God specifically gives human beings power over all other forms of life by nothing more than the force of his word.

97. The passage reinforces the notion that there are "natural" names for objects and that there is some language (presumably Hebrew) that is the "natural" language. This reaches the point where some people have the superstitious feeling that a dead language that lives on in a religious liturgy (Hebrew in the Jewish liturgy; Latin in the Roman Catholic) should be reserved for that and should not be profaned by ordinary use.

---

20 *And Adam gave names to all cattle, and to the fowl of the air, and to every beast of the field; but for Adam there was not found an help meet for him.*[98]

---

98. If we understand the last clause to mean that among all the animals of the land and air none was found to be a suitable partner for the man, that makes sense, since none are intelligent enough for the purpose.

Here, too, the J-document Creation-tale betrays its primitive nature. The Lord God is portrayed as experimenting—only after trying out the animals does he come to the conclusion that for a being as intelligent as a human being only another human being will do. The God of the P-document Creation-tale is at no time forced to experiment. All-knowing, he is depicted as creating the Universe as it should be.

If we insist on thinking of "help meet" as "wife," then we have the ludicrous picture of the Lord God bringing all the animals to the man to see if any of them will serve as wife. One might think that this alone would make it impossible to distort "help meet" in such a way, but the habit of not questioning the words of the Bible is a strong one.

---

21 *And the Lord God caused a deep sleep to fall upon Adam, and he slept:* [99] *and he took one of his ribs, and closed up the flesh instead thereof;*

---

99. This verse had an interesting connection with the history of science. When anesthesia was introduced in the mid-nineteenth century, there were some who felt that its use to reduce pain was a blasphemous attempt to avoid one of the punishments visited upon human beings by God. This verse was cited by physicians as an instance where God himself had used anesthesia when it was appropriate.

(This was not a completely convincing argument, for God's use of anesthesia took place before the man had been disobedient; the punishment of pain and of other unpleasantnesses came afterward. Still, the verse had its influence and made it a little easier for the use of anesthesia to be accepted.)

---

22 *And the rib, which the Lord God had taken from man, made he a woman, and brought her unto the man.*[100]

---

100. God forms the partner as not quite another man, but as a modified man; that is, a woman.

This amounts to the creation of sex in the J-document Creation-tale. Presumably, although the tale does not say so, all the animals are now provided with mates. After all, had God earlier provided mates for all animals when he formed them, he would not have been momentarily puzzled as to where to find a suitable partner for the man.

The P-document Creation-tale describes the creation of both sexes simultaneously. This is explicitly stated in the case of man and is implied in the case of the other animals, since God directed them all, "Be fruitful and multiply."

The J-document tells the more colorful tale, however, and most Bible readers ignore the more sophisticated account of the P-document and insist that woman was created after man and, what is more, out of a portion of man.

This is important because it encourages the belief that woman is a subsidiary being, created only as a partner for man in an afterthought, and that she is no more than an appendage of his (a rib) given human form.

If the woman were created after man in the P-document Creation-tale, that would indicate she was superior to man, for in the P-document creation moves up the scale, the best and most important coming last. In the J-document, however, the best and most important comes first, since plants and animals are created after man. Since woman is created last of all, that, too, seems to place a stamp of special inferiority upon her.

To be sure, ingenious interpretation can make it seem

that the J-document account preaches sexual equality, but in the last two thousand years and more, women have continually been considered the inferior sex on Biblical authority. One need only read Milton's great epic "Paradise Lost" to see male chauvinism of this type, naked and unashamed.

It is the P-document in this case that is closer to the scientific view of the history of life. Sexual reproduction is at least a billion years old, if not more, and the separation of sexes into separate individuals is probably nearly as old. In that separation, neither male nor female takes precedence.

In many species, particularly among the mammals, the male is physically larger and stronger than the female and can dominate in that way. This is not true of all animal species, however, not even of all mammalian species.

Physiologically, there are good reasons for arguing that the female is the more important and the male a mere adjunct. Among human beings, females have forty-six functioning chromosomes in each cell; males have forty-five plus a stub (the Y-chromosome). The male in this sense might be regarded as an incomplete and imperfect female, and it may be for this reason that females can better survive stress and have a life-span some six or seven years longer than males.

Then, too, while males and females contribute equally to the genetic equipment of the young, it is the female who contributes the initial food supply and generally supplies the postnatal care, if there is any. Among the mammals, the female supplies the environment within her own body for the initial stages of the growth of the young.

---

23 *And Adam said, This is now bone of my bones, and flesh of my flesh:* [101] *she shall be called Woman, because she was taken out of Man.* [102]

---

101. The formation of the woman out of the rib bears a distant resemblance to what we now think of as "cloning."

Of course, what God is described as doing in the Bible has a miraculous quality that cannot be legitimately compared to a mere human operation. For one thing, if a human being were cloned, the genetic character of the cells involved would make it certain that there would be no change in sex. The clone of a man would develop into a man, not into a woman. Similarly, the clone of a woman would develop into a woman, not into a man.

102. Here "Man" is a translation of the Hebrew word *ish,* which refers to the male of the species specifically, whereas *adam* is a more general term, closer to what we would think of as "human being." "Woman" is a translation of *ishshah,* which is a feminine form of *ish.* To call a woman *ishshah* is something like calling her a "Maness."

The word "woman," by the way, is not in itself a feminine form of "man," but is a corruption of the compound word "wife-man."

The fact that the man here gives a name to the woman is a further indication of his dominion over her.

---

24 *Therefore shall a man leave his father and his mother, and shall cleave unto his wife:* [103] *and they shall be one flesh.*

---

103. This verse can be used to signify that monogamy is the natural and original state of mankind. After all, the reference is to "wife" and not to "wives."

It is very likely, after all, that a monogamous relationship has always been common among human beings, since there are roughly equal numbers of each sex born. Therefore, if it is common for many men to be polygamous, it must mean that many other men must go without wives altogether, or that many women must be polyandrous.

Yet, whether monogamy is "natural" may be questioned. Many primate species are polygamous, and even among human beings there have been many cultures throughout history in which those who were wealthy enough or powerful enough collected as many wives as they could afford or could hold on to. Even where monogamy is enjoined by custom and by law, it seems almost impossible to suppress adultery, promiscuity, and prostitution.

Despite all this, monogamy may be desirable, but that doesn't mean it is natural.

---

25 *And they were both naked, the man and his wife, and were not ashamed.*[104]

---

104. Human beings are the only animals that deliberately cover their bodies with extraneous material for reasons associated with what we call "modesty." Other animals might cover themselves with mud in order to be cool or might make use of an unused shell for security, but as far as we know, only human beings are modest.

We can't be sure at what stage in the evolution of humanity the use of clothing developed. It seems to make sense to suppose that clothing was first worn to protect sensitive regions, such as the genitalia, from too rough a contact with the environment. (When human beings stood upright, the genital regions were even more exposed than they had been.)

Clothing may have become heavier and more enveloping when human beings migrated into cooler climates, where warmth was needed.

Clothes for the sake of modesty (or sometimes immodesty, as when articles of dress are used to accentuate the sexual regions) may have arisen as a by-product of these more utilitarian origins of the custom.

On the other hand, there are primitive cultures today in which nudity is not considered shameful, and even some advanced ones such as the Japanese or in nudist camps and beaches.

It seems reasonable to suppose that early in the history

of humanity, modesty had not been invented, and this verse, therefore, is a reasonable one.

And with this verse, the J-document Creation-tale comes to an end.

Chapter 3 [105]

---

1 *Now the serpent* [106] *was more subtil* [107] *than any beast of the field which the Lord God had made.* [108] *And he said* [109] *unto woman, Yea, hath God said, Ye shall not eat of every tree of the garden?* [110]

---

105. Here a new chapter starts, and appropriately so, for the Creation-tales are finished and primeval human history begins.

There is no indication how much time has elapsed after the woman was formed; we don't know whether Chapter 3 starts a day or a hundred years after the end of Chapter 2. For the purpose of the tale, the time doesn't matter, but the absence of time references is nevertheless inconvenient—at least to people in later ages who have learned to attach considerable importance to chronology.

106. The serpent enters the story. Apparently the tale that is about to be told is an adaptation of that portion of the Gilgamesh epic that dealt with how the serpent won its supposed immortality and how human beings lost theirs.

107. "Subtil" is an archaic spelling of "subtle." Later translations of the Bible characterize the serpent as "craftier" or "slyer" than other animals.

108. In actual fact, the snake is not an intelligent animal. It is a reptile, and reptiles are, in general, less intelligent than mammals. A snake seems crafty, however, because it slithers silently through the underbrush and

can attack before being seen; or, if it wishes to escape, it can vanish quickly into small openings. If that is not intelligence, it is, at any rate, a useful substitute.

A reference to the intelligence of serpents is found in the New Testament as well, where Jesus admonishes his apostles: "Behold, I send you forth as sheep in the midst of wolves: be ye therefore wise as serpents, and harmless as doves" (Matthew 10:16).

109. The serpent speaks. This, in itself, is an indication of the primitive nature of the tale of the Garden of Eden. It is one of only two instances in the Bible in which an animal speaks, the other being the case of Balaam's ass (Numbers 22:28-30). On the other hand, it may be that the serpent is more than a serpent.

110. The woman did not actually receive the Lord God's prohibition, for it was given to the man before the woman came into existence. To be sure, it might be argued that she was part of Adam's body at the time, but this is the same sort of argument as the one that explains, "In Adam's fall, we sinned all"—that Adam's fault spreads out over all his unborn descendants. Such arguments are by no means obviously acceptable, and many people don't accept them.

God might have repeated the instructions to Eve, but the Bible doesn't say so. Since the woman knows of the prohibitions, the likeliest explanation is that the man told her of it, and such a secondhand prohibition is never as forceful or as persuasive as the original. This could be considered as an extenuating point in favor of the woman, but it is not so considered either by God or by religionists who for thousands of years have held it bitterly against women that they, through the original woman, were the prime agents of the Fall and of the loss of immortality and innocence.

---

2 *And the woman said unto the serpent, We may eat of the fruit of the trees of the garden:*

3 *But of the fruit of the tree which is in the midst of the garden, God hath said, Ye shall not eat of it, neither shall ye touch it,[111] lest ye die.*

---

111. Here the woman enlarges and distorts the Lord God's instructions. God forbade only the eating of the fruit and said nothing, one way or the other, about touching it.

Some of the Rabbinic commentators suggest that it was this twisting of God's words that was the basic sin that led to all the rest. The legend they tell is that the serpent, on hearing the woman's version of the prohibition, shoved the woman against the tree, and when she suffered no harm as a result, she was ready to believe what the serpent had to say.

On the other hand, it might be argued that if the woman knew of the prohibition only indirectly, from what the man had told her, it might be conceivable that the man had distorted the instructions in the first place, perhaps in order to make it more forceful.

---

4 *And the serpent said unto the woman, Ye shall not surely die:* [112]

---

112. The serpent contradicts God. Why?

It seems motiveless, but the mere fact that the serpent does this gives us cause to suspect that it may be the principle of Chaos. In the Babylonian Creation-myth, Tiamat, the personification of Chaos, is described as a dragon, but a dragon is essentially a huge serpent, sometimes shown with wings (indicating perhaps the smoothness with which the serpent can slither here and there) and with fiery breath (indicating the serpent's poison).

Isaiah refers to all the terms used for Chaos when he promises the victory of God over the destructive forces: "In that day the Lord with his sore and great and strong sword shall punish leviathan the piercing serpent, even leviathan that crooked serpent; and he shall slay the dragon that is in the sea" (Isaiah 27:1).

In later times, when Judea was a province of the Persian Empire, the Jews picked up the notions of the eternal conflict between the principles of Good and Evil and abandoned the notions of a once-and-for-all victory of Good at the start.

Satan came into existence in Jewish thought as an eternal anti-God, striving constantly to undo the work of Creation and restore Chaos; eternal vigilance was required to prevent that. The thought then arose that the serpent was really the embodiment of Satan, a thought presented with unparalleled magnificence in Milton's "Paradise Lost."

There is, however, nothing in the Biblical story of the Garden of Eden to indicate that. The notion of Satan seems to have been entirely an afterthought.

---

5 *For God doth know that in the day ye eat thereof, then your eyes shall be opened, and ye shall be as gods,[113] knowing good and evil.*

---

113. There is a distant echo of the epic of Gilgamesh here. One character in the epic is Enkidu, a wild barbarian, and Gilgamesh must tame him. Gilgamesh uses a harlot for the purpose; she tempts him to sex with her beautiful body and her honeyed words, "Thou art beautiful, Enkidu; thou art like a god." She succeeds, and so does the tempting serpent, who promises the woman she shall be like a god.

---

6 *And when the woman saw that the tree was good for food, and that it was pleasant to the eyes, and a tree to be desired to make one wise, she took of the fruit thereof,[114] and did eat, and gave also unto her husband with her; and he did eat.*

---

114. The nature of the fruit is not mentioned. Traditionally, in the West, it was considered to have been an apple, but there is no warrant for that. In fact, we can be just about certain it wasn't an apple. Apples were not common and may not even have grown in ancient Palestine. If we want to take the tree of knowledge seriously, we would have to consider it a unique and possibly divine tree that could not have existed anywhere but in the Garden, and thus its fruit would not be within human ken except for that one sample eaten in disobedience.

From the prosaic standpoint of modern thought, the story is considered a legend and nothing more, and so the nature of the fruit is unimportant.

---

7 *And the eyes of them both were opened, and they knew that they were naked; and they sewed fig leaves together, and made themselves aprons.*[115]

---

115. The loss of innocence brought shame, and the man and woman sought to cover up their genitalia by making makeshift loincloths ("aprons"). It is because of this verse that the convention arose of carving leaves (usually referred to as fig leaves) over the male genitalia on statues. The pagan Greeks didn't do it, of course.

---

8 *And they heard the voice of the Lord God walking in the garden in the cool of the day: and Adam and his wife hid themselves from the presence of the Lord God amongst the trees of the garden.*

9 *And the Lord God called unto Adam, and said unto him, Where art thou?*

10 *And he said, I heard thy voice in the garden, and I was afraid, because I was naked; and I hid myself.*

11 *And he said, Who told thee that thou wast naked? Hast thou eaten of the tree, whereof I commanded thee that thou shouldest not eat?* [116]

---

116. This portion of the story is primitive indeed. God walks in the Garden, taking his constitutional when it is breezy, as a man might. The man and his wife hid, and God must call for them. God must ask if there had been disobedience, as if he were not all-knowing.

Later commentators, of course, explain these things in a variety of ways. The man and his wife hide because they are unaware of the powers of God, God asks the question only because he wishes a free confession, and so on.

And yet, in early myths, divine beings were not always all-knowing and were not even always very bright. Sometimes a clever man could get the better of a god. Perhaps, in the days before commentators, when the story was first told, listeners might have felt some suspense and wondered if the man would be able to worm his way out of the fix.

---

12 *And the man said, The woman whom thou gavest to be with me, she gave me of the tree, and I did eat.*

13 *And the Lord God said unto the woman, What is this that thou hast done? And the woman said, The serpent beguiled me, and I did eat.*

14 *And the Lord God said unto the serpent, Because thou hast done this, thou art cursed [117] above all cattle, and above every beast of the field; upon thy belly shalt thou go,[118] and dust shalt thou eat all the days of thy life:* [119]

---

117. God doesn't ask the serpent for an explanation, but condemns it unheard. Perhaps it is because this is the J-document's version of the battle between God and Chaos.

In the P-document, the battle was an utter victory for God, complete and instantaneous, when light was created and darkness retreated at God's word.

In the J-document, God wins again by a mere word in the form of the curse, but not till after Chaos had had its victory in upsetting the original plan of the man and his wife in the Garden. Later commentators had to avoid this appearance of God suffering even a partial defeat, however small, by making it appear that the Temptation and the Fall were part of God's original plan, but there is no clear sign of that anywhere in the Old Testament.

118. At no time does the Bible actually say the serpent walked on legs. The curse might well mean that the snake, which was created without legs, must now continue forever to lack them and to forfeit all chance whatever of someday gaining them as a reward for good behavior.

That, however, is not the way the passage is usually interpreted by readers of the Bible. It is almost universally supposed that the serpent did walk on legs until the curse compelled it to crawl upon its abdomen.

In a way, there is validity to this. It seems clear from the scientific view that snakes evolved from reptilian ancestors with the usual four legs and achieved their leglessness at least seventy-five million years ago. Nor was this a curse, though it may seem so to human beings. The long, thin bodies of snakes, their ability to hide in crannies and to creep along unseen, have made them by far the most successful group of present-day reptiles in the world.

One possible source for the tale of the curse rests again with the Babylonian dragon of Chaos. Babylon, at the time the Jews were exiled there, was at its peak of glory, the largest city in the world. Its walls were enormous and mighty, and the Ishtar gate, the chief entrance into the city, was decorated with large numbers of lions, bulls, and dragons (supposed to lend their symbolic strength to the city).

The dragons (called the *sirrush*) may well have been the dragon of Chaos. Some of those decorations still exist today on the ruins of the walls. The back, neck, and tail of the *sirrush* are clearly reptilian, though it is a quadruped like the lions and bulls. Cover up the legs of the *sirrush* and what is left is a serpent. It is easy to see, then, that the dragon of Chaos, cursed with leglessness, becomes a serpent.

119. Serpents, of course, do not eat dust. They are carnivorous creatures. The dust-eating is simply an overhasty conclusion from the position of their heads near the ground and from the constant flicking of their heat-sensitive tongues—a flicking that is not designed to lick up dust but to sense the near presence of some warm-blooded prey.

---

15 *And I will put enmity between thee and the woman, and between thy seed and her seed;* [120] *it shall bruise thy head and thou shalt bruise his heel.*[121]

---

120. Many people seem to have a horror of snakes. My own feeling is that we are so used to seeing mammals and birds in trees, in the air, or at the very least well above the ground that we don't generally inspect the ground itself for creatures above the size of insects. When a snake crosses our line of sight, therefore, we become conscious of movement where we are not expecting it and we have a "startle" reaction.

When snakes are on display in zoological gardens and are not in a position to be startled, we seem to watch snakes with equanimity, and even children are fascinated.

121. Taken literally, this section of the verse seems to make obvious sense. A human being trying to kill a snake

will surely aim at the head. A snake, on the ground, striking at a human being who is standing is likely to sink its fangs into the heel. It sounds as though it is an uneven fight, with the human being striking at a vital point while the snake cannot, and a human victory is implied. If the snake is poisonous, however, the fight is not as uneven as it seems. A strike at the heel can be deadly enough.

The apparent promise of human victory is sometimes taken as a Messianic prediction. A descendant of the woman ("her seed") is interpreted by Christians as Jesus Christ, and he will bruise the head of the serpent (Satan), thus bringing about the final victory over Chaos. It seems to take a convinced Christian to see this, however.

---

16 *Unto the woman he said, I will greatly multiply thy sorrow and thy conception; in sorrow thou shalt bring forth children;* [122] *and thy desire shall be to thy husband and he shall rule over thee.*[123]

---

122. The woman has not had children yet, and one wonders whether, if the man and woman had stayed in the Garden, they would ever have children. (If children *had* been born, presumably the process would have been easy and painless.)

One might argue that if the fruit of the tree had not been eaten, the man and woman would have continued to live in eternal bliss in the Garden. It was only after the fruit had been eaten and death had entered the world as an inevitable eventuality that the question of replacement arose.

This question arises only in the J-document. In the P-document Creation-tale, procreation exists from the beginning: all animals, and human beings in particular, are commanded to be fruitful and multiply. Under those circumstances, one might expect that death would be part of the life-scheme from the start, for ever-fruitful production of additional immortal creatures would quickly crowd the world unbearably.

Those one-celled forms of life that produce by simple division are, at least potentially, immortal. A virus can form replicas of itself endlessly. A bacterium, an alga, a protozoon can divide and redivide without cessation, and each cell formed in the divisions is as "young" as the original cell.

To be sure, one-celled organisms don't fill the Earth—as they assuredly would in a very short time, if they were all literally immortal—because vast numbers are constantly dying of starvation, of desiccation, of chemical pollution, and (mostly) of being eaten by somewhat larger organisms.

Multicellular organisms, on the other hand, are formed of anywhere from dozens to tens of trillions of various groups of specialized cells, and among them are the sex cells (eggs and sperm), which are entrusted with the task of reproducing new individuals.

Once there are sex cells for the job, the remainder of the organism tends to wear out in time even if the environment remains entirely favorable to life. We might say that the development of sex and of natural death came about simultaneously.

This is oddly akin to some allegorical interpretations of the tale of the serpent and the Temptation. Those who see the serpent as a symbol of the male genital organ would make it appear that the "forbidden fruit" was sexual experience. In that case, God was only pointing out the inevitable in saying that sex would mean death.

As for women bringing forth children "in sorrow," it would appear that women do have a difficult time of it in childbirth, more so than most animals do. This may be related to the rapid evolution of the human brain and to its tripling in size in the last half million years. The pelvic opening of the female has barely kept pace with this growth, and the head of the newborn infant, which is the largest part of the body and the first to emerge, does not slip through the pelvic opening easily. It is a tight fit.

Again, there is a rather interesting interpretation of the chapter that we can make. If the "forbidden fruit" of the "tree of knowledge" does represent knowledge, and since it is the growing brain that makes human knowledge possible, it makes a kind of sense to suppose that the pain of childbirth is the consequence of eating the fruit.

123. Presumably, despite the pains of childbirth, the sexual urge will force women to undergo the process.

The domination of women by men is a historical fact in most cultures, helped along by the fact that men are, on the average, larger and stronger than women are, and the further fact that women are periodically hampered by menstruation, pregnancy, lactation, and the need to take care of the young. Male domination is here justified as a punishment for the woman having been the first to yield to temptation.

This apparent Biblical sanction of male chauvinism, and this apparent Biblical condemnation of woman for her special and greater guilt, has, of course, been a source of much misery and unhappiness for women in those societies that accept the Bible as the inspired word of God.

---

17 *And unto Adam he said, Because thou hast hearkened unto the voice of thy wife, and hast eaten of the tree, of which I commanded thee, saying, Thou shalt not eat of it: cursed is the ground for thy sake; in sorrow shalt thou eat of it all the days of thy life;* [124]

---

124. This sounds very much like the sigh of a farmer. Humanity lived for many thousands of years by gathering food and by hunting. That came with labor enough, to be sure, for finding food was not easy, and in times of drought or of killing frosts, finding enough to feed all the mouths might well have been impossible.

When farming was developed, proper cultivation ensured a much larger food supply and it became possible to feed many more people on a given area of land. *However*, the labor of sowing, of weeding, of hoeing, of reaping, of guarding against predators meant backbreaking work. It must have seemed to many a weary farmer that the ground was cursed; that it had to be tended so carefully to produce the desired grain, for instance, and yet it so readily produced undesired, nonedible food.

If there was any dim recollection of the days of food-gathering, when all that work wasn't necessary, it might have been another factor that helped give rise to the tale of a fruitful paradise where all you had to do was pick a fruit and eat. It is very common for human beings to recall a past way of life with nostalgia and longing and to compare it favorably with a present way of life, simply by forgetting all the disadvantages of the past and by remembering (with a golden haze of improvements) the advantages.

---

18 *Thorns also and thistles shall it bring forth to thee; and thou shalt eat the herb of the field;* [125]

---

125. Despite the changed conditions, human beings are still restricted to a vegetarian diet. It is part of the punishment, apparently, that even though it would be harder to get food out of the ground, human beings must make do with it.

And it seems true that once human beings became farmers, grain became the staple food and vegetarian items formed a much greater component of the total diet than in the days before farming.

---

19 *In the sweat of thy face shalt thou eat bread, till thou return unto the ground; for out of it wast thou taken: for dust thou art, and unto dust shalt thou return.* [126]

---

126. This is the concept of recycling. We eat plants and animals and convert their tissues into our own. But then we die and decay, and our tissues are converted into the

tissues of other animals that may devour our bodies, or of lesser forms, worms, maggots, molds, bacteria that will live on the dead tissues. All those various life forms will in turn decay or be eaten, and the atoms and molecules of a once-living human body may well eventually form the tissues of another human body and be part of a living organism once more.

The Biblical writers knew nothing of microscopic life, but dust is not a bad way of describing it, in the absence of knowledge. Microorganisms are as small as dust grains, after all.

---

20 *And Adam called his wife's name Eve;* [127] *because she was the mother of all living.* [128]

---

127. It might be argued that now that human beings would die and be replaced by potentially endless numbers of other human beings, "man" and "woman" are insufficient as a means of identification. Each would need a proper name. The Revised Standard Version begins to use "Adam" instead of "the man" only in verse 3:17, when God pronounces Adam's doom.

And now Adam gives his wife a name. By doing so, he reinforces his control over her, which was granted him by God's dictum, four verses back.

128. "Eve" is the English form of the Hebrew *Chavah*. The actual meaning of the name is unknown (one suggestion is that it means "serpent"!), and it is probably not of Hebrew origin.

The ancient Israelites used names that meant something, however, and when they came across a name that was important to them and that didn't have an obvious meaning, they would use folk-etymological devices and find a meaning in a similar sound.

Thus, *Chavah* has a sound similar to *Chayah* which means "life" in Hebrew. The Biblical writers therefore suggest that she was called Eve because she was the human source of all subsequent human life.

116

21 Unto Adam also and to his wife did the
Lord God make coats of skins, and clothed
them.[129]

129. This is a primitive element of the story, since one
gets the picture of God sewing skins together and becoming a tailor as well as a potter. Worse yet, one gets the
picture of God killing and skinning animals.

It is easy to suppose that God merely created the
clothing of skins as easily as he created Adam, without
having to kill animals for the purpose, but the verse
doesn't make that clear.

It does make sense to suppose that clothing of skins
did come after clothing made of leaves. It is considerably
more difficult to catch and skin animals than to pick
leaves. On the other hand, it is worth the added effort,
for skins offer better protection to delicate parts of the
body and offer additional insulation against the cold,
something useful and even necessary once human beings
moved out of the tropics.

22 And the Lord God said, Behold, the man is
become as one of us,[130] to know good and
evil: [131] and now, lest he put forth his
hand, and take also of the tree of life, and
eat, and live for ever: [132]

130. Here is another indication of a primitive polytheism that the Biblical writers somehow let stand.

131. The serpent had told Eve that if she ate of the fruit
of the tree of knowledge, she would become like a god,
and here God himself seems to agree.

132. This would seem to be the most primitive portion
of the entire tale of the Garden of Eden. Adam and Eve
were, presumably, immortal before they ate the fruit of
the tree, but they were no threat to God then, for they

lacked wisdom. Even after they gained wisdom and became "as one of us," they were still no threat to God for they were now mortal.

If, however, having gained wisdom, they also ate of the fruit of the tree of life and regained their immortality, they would, perhaps, become a threat. Wisdom and immortality together would be too much, and we have an odd picture of a *timorous* God.

It might be argued that God was not afraid of even a wise and immortal human being but merely did not want Adam to become immortal and override God's edict of mortality for him. In that case, we have the equally odd picture of a God who can be overridden.

However interpreted, this part of the story must date back to an earlier time when gods were much more human and possessed human failings (like the gods in Homer's epics) and before the priestly writers of the Babylonian period had drawn the picture of a transcendent and omnipotent God.

---

23 *Therefore the Lord God sent him forth from the garden of Eden, to till the ground from whence he was taken.*

24 *So he drove out the man; and he placed at the east of the garden of Eden Cherubims,[133] and a flaming sword which turned every way [134] to keep the way of the tree of life.[135]*

---

133. The entities serving as guardians are, in the singular, "cherub." The Hebrew method of forming a plural is to add the suffix *-im*, so that more than one cherub are *cherubim*. The King James Version adds the English plural "-s" suffix, making a double plural out of it. The Revised Standard Version has it simply "cherubim."

The Biblical writers do not define cherubim nor do they describe them. They are mentioned elsewhere in the Bible, and about all we can obtain clearly is that they are winged and probably fearsome creatures.

It may be that the cherubim are symbolic of storms and might be viewed as storm demons. Early man found storms fearsome and threatening (as we do today) and was all too prone to view storms as the direct activity of an angry and raging deity. The wind is invisible and has a superhuman strength, and both are godlike attributes.

The "Spirit of God" referred to in Genesis 1:2 is a visualization of God as a wind stirring the waters of chaos. If God were angry, the wind that represents him might become a raging storm.

Thus, in Psalms 18:6-15, the anger of God is visualized as a convulsion of nature: earthquakes, volcanoes, and storms. The tenth verse reads: "And he rode upon a cherub, and did fly: yea, he did fly upon the wings of the wind."

134. If the cherubim are storm demons then the flaming sword which turned every way might well be the lightning.

135. The implication is that the Garden of Eden, or the "Earthly Paradise," as some call it, still exists, but that it is shrouded and hidden behind perpetual storm clouds and that anyone approaching would be struck down by lightning.

It was common in many ancient mythologies to suppose that some land or island existed in some unknown and distant spot where all troubles ceased and happiness reigned supreme. The Elysian Fields of the ancient Greeks was one such place. The Isle of Avalon in the legends of King Arthur is another.

In medieval times, the Earthly Paradise took on the aspects of such a place, and it seemed easy to suppose it to be still existing in some far corner of the globe—so little of which was known to medieval Europeans. Dante, in his *Divine Comedy*, put it at the top of the mountain of Purgatory, which he located at that point on the globe directly opposite to Jerusalem. (The point opposite to Jerusalem is, actually, located in the South Pacific at a point about 800 miles northeast of the northern tip of New Zealand.)

Now that Earth has been thoroughly explored, it is clear that the Earthly Paradise does not exist upon its surface. Still, to those who do not choose to abandon it, it would not be difficult to maintain that it has been spirited to another planet, or to Heaven—or even that it exists on Earth but is, thanks to the guardian cherubim, invisible to human sight.

Chapter 4

---

1 *And Adam knew* [136] *Eve his wife; and she conceived, and bare Cain,* [137] *and said, I have gotten a man from the Lord.* [138]

---

136. This is a Biblical euphemism for sexual relations. The Bible is full of euphemisms. The use of "Lord" in place of "Yahveh" is a euphemism, for that matter.

137. The name Cain (*Kayin* in Hebrew) means "smith."
In the early days of civilization, the use of metals was introduced, and the new materials became exceedingly important both in ornamentation and in the manufacture of tools and of weapons for hunting and warfare. Men who could prepare the metals and work them into the necessary shapes were important and highly regarded artisans. To be a smith and to be called one was a matter of pride and honor, and to this day Smith is a common surname among English-speaking peoples.

138. To explain the name, the Biblical writers sought for some similar-sounding Hebrew word and found it in *kanah,* meaning "to get."

---

2 *And she again bare his brother Abel.* [139] *And Abel was a keeper of sheep,* [140] *but Cain was a tiller of the ground.* [141]

---

139. No derivation is given for the name Abel *(Hebel* or *Hevel* in Hebrew). The Hebrew word means "nothingness," and this is taken usually to represent the briefness of Abel's life. The actual derivation, however, may be *aplu,* which is an Akkadian word for "son."

140. Since human beings were as yet allowed to eat only vegetable life, one might wonder why Abel kept sheep. Presumably, only for the production of wool and the fashioning of garments therefrom. If so, this is not likely to match actual history. As far as we know, the first herdsmen used their animals as a food supply in addition to any other uses involved.

141. Farming and herding grew up together in the early days of civilization, but since plants can be grown more thickly than animals, and since more calories per acre can be produced in the form of cultivated grain than in the form of domesticated animals, farming communities were more thickly populated than herding communities.

The larger population of agricultural societies offered more opportunity for specialization and for technological advance, so that the use of metals (as well as of other luxuries) was more associated with the settled and populous farming communities than with the roaming, sparsely peopled herding tribes. It is rather appropriate, therefore, that the farmer should be named Cain ("smith").

---

3 *And in process of time it came to pass, that Cain brought of the fruit of the ground an offering unto the Lord.*[142]

---

142. This is the first example of a sacrificial rite in the Bible. The word "sacrifice" is from the Latin, meaning "to make sacred," that is, to set aside something for the use of a god. Because one deprives one's self in order to set aside something for the gods, "sacrifice" has gained its present meaning.

Originally, the motivation that led to the sacrifice may well have been analogous to that which leads to the bringing of a gift to a king. It is a sign of devotion and loyalty—and also a way of putting him into a good mood or even inspiring him with a feeling of friendship and gratitude. It's the apple-for-the-teacher gambit.

Quite likely, the original notion was that gods ate, too. If food is burned, the rising smoke would carry the essence of the food upward to where the gods were thought to live, and in grateful exchange the gods would grant a good harvest or victory over one's enemies.

In later times, of course, the reasons for sacrifice were made more lofty, but the practice was eventually abandoned just the same.

---

4 *And Abel, he also brought of the firstlings of his flock and of the fat thereof.*[143] *And the Lord had respect unto Abel and to his offering.*

---

143. Presumably Abel killed the firstborn lambs ("firstlings") for the sacrifice, which would seem to indicate that though human beings had been directed to be vegetarians, God himself remained carnivorous.

---

5 *But unto Cain and to his offering he had not respect.*[144] *And Cain was very wroth, and his countenance fell.*

---

144. The Bible does not say at this point in what way God showed respect or why he favored Abel over Cain. Later commentators maintained that Cain was wicked, that he offered his sacrifices reluctantly, that he chose undesirable portions of the harvest—while Abel was good, chose the best lambs, and offered them gladly. Or, as is stated in the New Testament (see Hebrews 11:4), Abel had faith and Cain did not, and therefore Abel's sacrifice was superior.

The story in Genesis says none of these things, however, and the most direct interpretation might be that the sacrifice of animals was superior to that of grain. In a way, this makes sense, since animal food was more expensive than plant food (and still is, as you know) and therefore would represent a more valuable sacrifice. Besides that, animals were regarded as living and plants were not, and so living things were a more valuable gift to God than nonliving things could be. (In many forms of primitive worship, the most valuable sacrifice of all was that of a human being.) This would make it look as though God favored Abel over Cain because Abel offered the greater bribe, so to speak.

On the other hand, the story of Cain and Abel is an old legend that the Israelites may well have told when they were still nomadic herdsmen wandering in the Arabic borderlands and before they had settled down in the land of Canaan. Abel the shepherd would naturally be the hero of the tale, and Cain the farmer would be the villain. Herding ways would be considered superior to farming ways, and the sacrifices of the herdsman superior to those of the farmer.

---

6 *And the Lord said unto Cain, Why art thou wroth? and why is thy countenance fallen?*

7 *If thou doest well, shalt thou not be accepted? and if thou doest not well, sin lieth at the door. And unto thee shall be his desire, and thou shalt rule over him.*[145]

---

145. This verse in the King James Version is rather obscure. The Revised Standard Version has the verse read: "If you do well, will you not be accepted? And if you do not do well, sin is couching at the door; its desire is for you, but you must master it."

This seems to recognize the wickedness in Cain, but it is the conditional that is used—the possibility that Cain will do something wrong in the future. It may be considered as implying that he has already done something wrong in the past, and that was why God lacked respect for his sacrifice—but the Bible doesn't say so.

This is the first verse in which the word "sin" is used. "Sin" is a translation of a Hebrew word that can mean "deviation from the terms of an agreement" or "rebellion." If Cain puts himself into an ugly frame of mind, the temptation of rebelling against the dictates of God will arise, and he must master that temptation.

---

8 *And Cain talked with Abel his brother: and it came to pass, when they were in the field, that Cain rose up against Abel his brother, and slew him.*[146]

---

146. From the earliest days of farming, there was war between the settled agricultural communities and the nomad tribes on the fringes.

As time went on, agricultural communities gathered in surpluses of food, ornaments, tools, weapons; and herdsmen, condemned to travel constantly in search of fresh pasture for their animals, could not do so. The wealth of the settled communities was a standing temptation for the nomadic herdsmen.

As a consequence, settled communities were forever fighting off "barbarian raids." The last and greatest of these, which founded the relatively short-lived Mongol Empire, devastated various parts of Asia from 1225 to 1265. Eastern Europe was overrun in 1240 and 1241.

Histories are usually written by the intellectuals of settled societies. It's no surprise, then, that the nomads are pictured as cruel, destructive, and murderous. And yet it is usually the nomads who get the worst of it and suffer the more.

The settled agricultural communities have the more advanced weapons and can hide behind city walls. In general, the armies of civilization are more numerous and better armed, and when well led they can usually destroy the barbarians. (After the Mongol invasions, the coming of gunpowder put the weight of strength permanently on the side of civilization, and the nomads were permanently crushed.)

Nomads sometimes do successfully invade a civilized region and take it over, but this happens only at times when, for one reason or another, the civilized region has decayed or has disintegrated into civil war. The story of Cain and Abel is one of the very few well-known literary fragments in western literature that tell the tale from the viewpoint of the nomad who, in the long run, was destroyed by the farmer.

---

9 *And the Lord said unto Cain, Where is Abel thy brother? And he said, I know not: Am I my brother's keeper?*

10 *And he said, What hast thou done? the voice of thy brother's blood [147] crieth unto me from the ground.*

---

147. Primitive societies quite reasonably attach a great deal of importance to blood. It could be argued that it represented a principle of life as important as that of the breath. If an animal's throat is cut so that it bleeds freely, it weakens as it bleeds and eventually dies, as though life left it along with the blood; as though life and blood were the same. This equivalent of life and blood is specifically stated in various verses of the Bible.

The Bible does not say just how Cain slew Abel. Had it been by strangulation or by a blow on the head, life would have departed without blood having been spilled. (The fact that death may come without the loss of a single drop of blood is an argument against the absolute equation of life and blood.)

The implication here, however, is that blood seeped into the ground, and it seems logical to suppose that Cain, the "smith," used a spear, an arrow, a knife—some penetrating, cutting weapon that would signify the superior technology of the civilized man as against the nomad.

In that case, life would not so much be lost as transferred. The blood, still alive by its very nature, would from the ground call out to God.

---

11 *And now art thou cursed from the earth, which hath opened her mouth to receive thy brother's blood from thy hand;*

12 When thou tillest the ground, it shall not henceforth yield unto thee her strength; a fugitive and a vagabond shalt thou be in the earth.[148]

---

148. This is apparently another ancient tradition that has been grafted onto the preceding one, because this one also involves nomads.

In the first story, the tale of the hostility of farmers and nomads is told from the nomad viewpoint. The wicked farmer kills, without cause, the virtuous shepherd.

Now we have an explanation, however, from the farmer's point of view, of what nomads are and how they came to be. Cain is now forced to cease being a farmer and to become a nomad. The implication is that nomads are what they are because they are criminals by nature and incapable of forming part of a decent, law-abiding, settled society.

---

13 *And Cain said unto the Lord, My punishment is greater than I can bear.*

14 Behold, thou hast driven me out this day from the face of the earth; and from thy face shall I be hid; and I shall be a fugitive and a vagabond in the earth; and it shall come to pass, that every one [149] that findeth me shall slay me.

---

149. Who is the "every one"? If we have been following the tale of Adam and Eve and accept the common assumption that they were the only living human beings

at the time of the Garden of Eden, then the total population of Earth at the time of the murder of Abel was three:
Adam, Eve, and Cain.

Could it be that Adam and Eve had many children,
who have gone unnamed and unmentioned but now pop-
ulate the world? Could it be a reference to the various
animals, some powerful and predatory, that exist in the
world?

Could it be that the Creation-myths of the P-document
and the J-document refer to two different sets of the
works of God? Perhaps God created human beings, male
and female, many of them on the sixth day of Creation,
and they filled the Earth. Afterward, it may be, he created Adam and Eve, alone in the Garden, as the progeni-
tors of a particular family. Thus, Cain would now fear
death at the hands of any of the numerous "pre-Adamites."

None of this is made plain by the Bible. It may be that
the tale of Adam and Eve ("how death came into the
world," we might call it) ends with the expulsion from
Eden. What follows next would be various legends dealing with primeval history and the birth of civilization, all
of which are linked together, rather clumsily, by the Biblical writers.

There is one story of how crime came into being, and a
second dealing with how the nomadic way of life came
into being. Both presuppose a world full of people, and it
is only the attachment to the Adam and Eve tale, by making Cain and Abel their sons, that creates confusion.

---

15 *And the Lord said unto him, Therefore
whosoever slayeth Cain, vengeance shall
be taken on him sevenfold. And the Lord
set a mark upon Cain,*[150] *lest any finding
him should kill him.*

---

150. It doesn't seem to make sense to protect Cain so
zealously after the unprovoked murder he committed,
unless we suppose that a life of exile and wandering is
greater punishment than immediate death. On the other

hand we are now into the primeval history tale, and this verse may be intended to account for the habit of some nomadic tribes of marking themselves with characteristic tattoos.

Agricultural societies eventually develop a more or less complex system of laws that are finally committed to writing and a complex judicial system to interpret and enforce those laws. The simpler society of the nomads, however, lacks such a written law and must do without.

Where laws are not carefully defined and their exact wording is not available, there is less security. Where there is not a set and proper machinery for dealing with lawbreakers, the law of the vigilante is put into motion. Summary justice at the hands of a mob becomes the rule.

Thus, if a member of a tribe is murdered by an outsider, the rest of the tribe is duty-bound to hunt down the murderer and kill him. Presumably, the sure knowledge that murder will bring down retaliation upon the murderer is a powerful incentive against such crimes of violence.

Naturally, the member of a numerous and powerful tribe will want to be sure that everyone who casually encounters him knows that he is not someone who might be harmed with impunity. The tribesman therefore wears his tribal tattoo (as a modern traveler carries a passport) as identification.

In later times, there was the tribe of Kenites, who were not Israelites but who lived in close association with the tribe of Judah (see Judges 1:16). The Kenites were a nomadic tribe of whom Cain was the eponymous ancestor (a real or mythical individual from whom a tribe or a people takes its name).

This portion of the Cain legend may be a fragment of a Kenite tale about how the tribal tattoo-mark came into being, although we may suppose that the Kenites did not portray their ancestor as a murderer.

---

16 *And Cain went out from the presence of the Lord, and dwelt in the land of Nod,[151] on the east of Eden.*

---

151. There is no land known as Nod. The word, in Hebrew, means "wandering," so that to say that Cain "dwelt in the land of Nod" would seem to be a metaphorical way of saying that he became a wanderer, a nomad.

"Nomad," by the way, has nothing to do with "Nod." Nomad is from a Greek word meaning "to seek for pasture."

---

17 And Cain knew his wife; [152] and she conceived, and bare Enoch: and he builded a city,[153] and called the name of the city, after the name of his son, Enoch.[154]

---

152. Where did Cain get his wife?

A common assumption is that Adam and Eve had daughters as well as sons but that daughters routinely went unmentioned in the Bible. In that case, Cain married his sister, a case of incest there was no way of avoiding. (After all, Adam married his own clone.)

Another possibility is the one mentioned in connection with Cain's fear of being killed as an outlaw—that numerous pre-Adamites existed and that Cain married one of those.

It is most reasonable to suppose that the legends of Cain deal with a primordial already-populated world, and that the legends were artificially connected to the Adam-and-Eve story, thus creating difficulties.

153. Immediately after Cain is described as taking up a wandering life in accordance with the avenging word of God, he settles down to build a city. Apparently, we are back to Cain, the farmer, of the first eight verses of the chapter.

Farming communities inevitably built cities, since the farmers had to huddle together for protection. Unlike herdsmen, they could not move about; they could not drive their herds ahead of them and move away whenever conditions seemed to grow insecure. They were nailed to the spot by their farms and had to protect those farms and themselves.

To have Cain, the farmer, build a city, therefore, makes sense. Naturally, to build a city implies a population. Even a very small and very primitive city would have a couple of hundred people in it. Therefore, those who are puzzled by the identity of Cain's wife would do better to puzzle over the identity of the people who populated Cain's city.

154. There is no city we know of in very early times by the name of Enoch, or anything recognizably like it. Nor is the city referred to elsewhere in the Bible.

In actual history, one of the oldest cities to be founded (or even, perhaps, the very oldest) is a city well known to the Biblical writers. It was Jericho, located twenty-five kilometers (fifteen miles) northeast of Jerusalem and frequently mentioned in the Bible. It may have come into existence about 8000 B.C.

There is absolutely no reason to suppose, however, that Enoch represents Jericho.

---

18 *And unto Enoch was born Irad: and Irad begat Mehujael: and Mehujael begat Methusael: and Methusael begat Lamech.*[155]

---

155. The Biblical writers are interested in genealogies for three reasons.

First, family relationships of all degrees are important in tribal societies. Genealogies serve to fit various individuals into appropriate slots.

Second, genealogies fill up gaps. Those portions of history concerning which nothing of interest (or even nothing at all) can be related are quickly disposed of by simply listing a line of descent.

Third, genealogies are a way of quickly describing and being done with the history of a tribe or group of tribes that is not ancestral to the Israelites (with whom the Biblical story primarily deals). Cain and his progeny are thus disposed of, since none of them are in the line of Israelite ancestry.

Because of the free use in the King James Version of the word "begat," meaning "procreated" or "sired" (not really "gave birth to" since that is the prerogative of the female of the species), such passages are colloquially known as "the begats." The word is eliminated in the Revised Standard Version, which has the verse read: "To Enoch was born Irad; and Irad was the father of Mehujael; and Mehujael the father of Methusael, and Methusael the father of Lamech."

---

19 *And Lamech took unto him two wives:* [156] *the name of the one was Adah, and the name of the other Zillah.* [157]

---

156. This is the first mention of polygamy in the Bible, and there is no clear indication that it is viewed with disapproval, either here or in any of the other historical books of the Bible prior to the Babylonian exile.

157. These are the first women named in the Bible—or even mentioned—since Eve. All through the Bible there is a vast disproportion in the number of men and women mentioned, as there is in non-Biblical histories. The world has long concerned itself with men almost exclusively.

---

20 *And Adah bare Jabal: he was the father of such as dwell in tents, and of such as have cattle.* [158]

---

158. Here we have a brief reference to another legend concerned with the beginnings of herding, which eighteen verses earlier had been attributed to Abel. The names of Abel and Jabal are sufficiently similar, how-

ever, to make one wonder whether the two accounts are not different versions of the same legend. (Again one must ask as to the uses of herding where human beings are restricted to a vegetarian diet. One answer might be for skins, leather, and wool for clothing. Of course, one might also argue that the line of Cain broke the divine edict in line with the growing sinfulness of humanity— but the Bible doesn't say so directly.)

---

21 *And his brother's name was Jubal: he was the father of all such as handle the harp and organ.*

22 *And Zillah, she also bare Tubal-cain,[159] an instructer of every artificer in brass [160] and iron [161]: and the sister of Tubal-cain was Naamah.[162]*

---

159. The mention of Tubal-cain strengthens the possibility that we have here a second version of the same legend given at the beginning of the chapter. At the start of the chapter we have two brothers—Abel, the herdsman, and Cain, the farmer. Here we have Jabal, the herdsman, and Tubal-cain, the metallurgist. This time around there is no conflict or murder described; the Bible concentrates on the two as "culture-heroes," that is, as originating some line of human activity.

160. The Hebrew word *nehosheth* is translated as "brass" in the King James Version. More correctly, it should be translated as "copper" or "bronze." The earliest use of copper for ornamentation was soon after 4000 B.C. Alloyed with arsenic or tin, copper could be made hard enough to be used in tools or weapons, and this alloy was called bronze. By 3000 B.C. bronze was coming into use. By Biblical standards, the period 4000–3000 B.C. was the dawn of history, so the association of copper with Tubal-cain is reasonable.

161. The name Tubal-cain means "smith of Tubal," Tubal being a district in Asia Minor on the southeast shore of the Black Sea. As a matter of fact, the techniques of iron smelting and ironworking were first developed in the neighborhood of that region, so the association of Tubal-cain with iron is a good one.

However, iron was first smelted about 1300 B.C., and it did not come into general use for some centuries afterward. To lump iron with copper in the time of Tubal-cain is an anachronism.

162. This chapter, which is part of the J-document, lists eight generations, starting with Adam: (1) Adam, (2) Cain, (3) Enoch, (4) Irad, (5) Mehujael, (6) Methusael, (7) Lamech, and (8) Lamech's children.

There were lists of early kings in the Tigris-Euphrates region concerning whom nothing was reported but their names. A very early list compiled by the Sumerians listed eight names, but these names are very different from those in this chapter. Conceivably, as the legends were told and retold, the Sumerian names may have been altered to Hebrew equivalents in a folk-etymological manner and ended up in the J-document as we now have them.

---

23 *And Lamech* [163] *said unto his wives, Adah and Zillah, Hear my voice; ye wives of Lamech, hearken unto my speech: for I have slain a man to my wounding, and a young man to my hurt.*[164]

---

163. Lamech seems to have importance. He has two wives, three sons, and a daughter, all of whom are named, even the daughter. And now a short poem is about to be attributed to him. Lamech may have been a Kenite folk-hero, and some of the deeds attributed to him are borrowed by the J-document, perhaps because tales of him were so popular in Judah that he had to be incorporated into the Judean account of primeval history.

164. The second part of the verse is obscure in the King James Version. The Revised Standard Version has it read, "I have slain a man for wounding me, a young man for striking me."

The reference is probably to a single feat of killing. Hebrew poetry achieves its effects very often by "parallelism"; that is, by saying the same thing in two slightly different ways. The J-document may here be incorporating an old Kenite war song.

---

24 *If Cain shall be avenged sevenfold, truly Lamech seventy and sevenfold.*[165]

---

165. Lamech seems jubilant over his victory, indicating that he considers his killing to be superior to that of Cain. Perhaps (the Bible doesn't say, of course) he was thinking that Cain slew an unprepared and unarmed man, while he himself may have killed an armed man in a duel.

Certainly, this would seem to be an indication that in the course of the eight generations from Adam, human conflict had progressed from individual fighting to organized war. There seems to be a continued moral deterioration of humanity after the expulsion from the Garden, at least in the line of Cain.

With this victory song as climax and as evidence of degradation, the J-document leaves the descendants of Cain at this point. They are abandoned as unsuitable to be discussed further. The tale turns to another line descended from Adam.

---

25 *And Adam knew his wife again; and she bare a son, and called his name Seth: For God, said she, hath appointed* [166] *me another seed instead of Abel, whom Cain slew.*

---

166. The name Seth sounds like the Hebrew word for "appointed" or "granted," so that Eve is made to give him the name in a folk-etymological manner.

---

26 *And to Seth, to him also there was born a son; and he called his name Enos:* [167] *then began men to call upon the name of the Lord.*[168]

---

167. The two brothers, Cain and Seth, had sons of similar names: Enoch and Enos (in Hebrew *Hannoch* and *Enosh*). It may be that the descendants of Seth are also derived from the Sumerian king-lists, so that the two lines of descent from Adam, by way of Cain and by way of Seth, represent two different versions of the Sumerian sources.

168. This would seem to mean that instead of worshipping a nameless god or some false one, people in the time of Enos began to worship Yahveh. According to the J-document, at least, this would indicate the beginning of Yahvism (out of which Judaism, Christianity, and Islam all developed).

The J-document, in this chapter, thus clearly distinguishes between the two lines of descent from Adam. The line of Cain was marked by murder, polygamy, the development of metal weapons, and warfare. The line of Seth, on the other hand (from which the Israelites were descended, by the Biblical account), was marked by the development of true religion.

Chapter 5

1 *This is the book of the generations of Adam.*[169] *In the day that God*[170] *created man, in the likeness of God made he him;*

169. This is an introductory phrase that introduces a new section; one that bears little connection with what has immediately preceded.

170. The use of "God" instead of "the Lord" or "Lord God" shows that we are back in the P-document after three chapters of J-document.

2 *Male and female created he them; and blessed them,*[171] *and called their name Adam,*[172] *in the day when they were created.*

171. The P-document harks back to the point where it left off at the beginning of Chapter 2. It skips over the whole tale of the Garden of Eden, of Eve and the serpent, of Cain and Abel, of the descendants of Cain. It does not deal with them and, apparently, knows nothing of them.

172. The P-document again emphasizes the simultaneous creation of man and woman. It is not only the male who is called Adam ("man"), but both of them. Here the word *adam* is equivalent to "mankind" or "humanity." It is still possible that a large number of men and women were created.

3 *And Adam* [173] *lived an hundred and thirty years,*[174] *and begat a son in his own likeness, after his image;* [175] *and called his name Seth:*

173. Now Adam is spoken of as an individual, but this does not necessarily mean that, in the P-document, only one man was created to begin with. We merely shift from mankind in general to one particular man from whom the line of the Israelites had its beginnings.

174. The J-document, in listing the descendants of Cain, gives no ages or time durations. The priestly writers of the P-document are more meticulous in these details.

175. The P-document makes no mention of Cain and Abel. If we consider the P-document only, Seth is the firstborn of Adam. This could explain the reference to "a son in his own likeness, after his image."

In Genesis 1:26, we have "And God said, Let us make man in our image, after our likeness." This could, conceivably, have applied only to the man and woman (or the men and women) directly created by God. By pointing out that Seth was born in Adam's "own likeness, after his image," and therefore in God's, the indication would be that all Adam's descendants and, therefore, all human beings are in God's image. At least this would be true of all those of the line of Seth, and as we shall see later, that includes all of mankind.

Another possibility is that Seth may here be differentiated from the wicked Cain and his descendants. Cain was not in the image of Adam and therefore of God, but in that case, what about the virtuous Abel? It probably makes more sense not to try to mix the P-document and the J-document.

4 *And the days of Adam after he had begotten Seth were eight hundred years: and he begat sons and daughters:* [176]

---

176. If Adam sired children as often as we do and had eight hundred years to do it in, he could easily have fathered four hundred sons and four hundred daughters. If each of these were equally long-lived and equally prolific, then in a mere four generations, twenty-five billion people would have been born.

In actual fact, the population of Earth in 3500 B.C. (roughly the time of the immediate generations after Adam, according to the traditional chronology) was about ten million—something that could easily have been managed if long-lived individuals had followed God's blessing and edict that they "be fruitful and multiply, and replenish the earth."

It might also solve some problems, since if Cain were equally long-lived, he needed only to wait some centuries, and then there would be plenty of people from among whom to choose a wife and with whom to build a city and, for that matter, from whom to expect harm.

In exchange, of course, we are faced with the problem of accounting for these long life-spans.

The P-document does not name the sons and daughters that Adam sired after Seth. It does the same in connection with each descendant in this chapter, naming only one son and ignoring all other children. It is the named sons who are the ancestors of the Israelites. All other lines of descent will not survive a coming catastrophe, and they are therefore ignored.

---

5 *And all the days that Adam lived were nine hundred and thirty years;* [177] *and he died.*

177. Adam and his descendants, according to the P-document (at least those descendants who are given names in this chapter), had extended lifetimes, living far longer than what we now recognize to be the maximum life-span of the human being (about 115 years).

As one progresses through the Bible, the life-span of human beings is described as gradually decreasing until, by the end of the Book of Genesis, 150 is recognized as extreme old age, and by the time of King David seventy is.

Could it be that early man lived long and that modern man's short life-span is an example of degeneracy?

From the scientific standpoint, this is probably the reverse of the truth. *Homo sapiens* always had the capacity to live for a hundred years or a little more (a longer life-span than that of any other mammal), but in early time he almost never had the chance to do so. Life was brutal and chancy, and few people lived past forty. This was true right down to the middle of the nineteenth century.

Throughout historic times, there were cases of human beings living to be over ninety, according to reliable report—Sophocles in the fifth century B.C., Isocrates in the fourth century B.C., Cassiodorus in the sixth century, Titian in the sixteenth century, and so on—but they were comparatively few in number.

It was only after modern medicine was developed and infectious disease could be controlled that the *average* life-span began to increase.

Once people reach the age of sixty, it is the degenerative diseases that take their toll (cancer, arthritis, heart attack, strokes, kidney failure, and so on). These have not yet yielded to the blandishments of medicine, so that a man of sixty today has little more in the way of life expectancy than a man of sixty in the times of Sophocles, twenty-four hundred years ago. Of course, many more reach the age of sixty now than in those times.

If so, then how explain the extended life-spans of Adam and his immediate descendants?

Some have suggested that the "years" here given are really lunar months, since the calendar had not yet been extended to include the solar years. There are twelve and a third lunar months in a year, so that if Adam lived for 930 lunar months, that would be equivalent to about seventy-six years, which sounds right.

However, the ages given for the time of the birth of the oldest son would then become absurdly low and the ages of later descendants who live for shorter and shorter periods of time become hard to interpret.

The most likely explanation rests with the Sumerian king-lists. For each of the early kings there is given the number of years he reigned, and these are invariably in the tens of thousands of years. Two are described as reigning 64,800 years each.

The writers of the P-document would not accept that. They were willing to believe extended lifetimes, but within limits. All the descendants of Adam, as well as Adam himself, are carefully given life-spans of less than a thousand years. The P-document, in short, is being conservative.

The life-spans of these descendants of Adam are an important factor in calculating the traditional year in which the Creation took place. The result (so often given as 4004 B.C.), while useless for the creation of Earth or the birth of humanity, is a fairly reasonable estimate for the beginning of the Sumerian civilization.

---

6 And Seth lived an hundred and five years, and begat Enos:

7 And Seth lived after he begat Enos eight hundred and seven years, and begat sons and daughters:

8 And all the days of Seth were nine hundred and twelve years: and he died.

9 And Enos lived ninety years, and begat Cainan: [178]

---

178. Cainan (or Kenan, as the name is given in the Revised Standard Version) could be the P-document's version of the J-document's Cain.

10 *And Enos lived after he begat Cainan eight hundred and fifteen years, and begat sons and daughters:*

11 *And all the days of Enos were nine hundred and five years: and he died.*

12 *And Cainan lived seventy years and begat Mahalaleel:* [179]

179. Mahalaleel could be the P-document's version of the J-document's Mehujael.

13 *And Cainan lived after he begat Mahalaleel eight hundred and forty years, and begat sons and daughters:*

14 *And all the days of Cainan were nine hundred and ten years: and he died.*

15 *And Mahalaleel lived sixty and five years, and begat Jared:* [180]

180. Jared could be the P-document's version of the J-document's Irad.

16 *And Mahalaleel lived after he begat Jared eight hundred and thirty years, and begat sons and daughters:*

17 *And all the days of Mahalaleel were eight hundred ninety and five years: and he died.*

18 *And Jared lived an hundred sixty and two years, and he begat Enoch:* [181]

181. Here is a name that is identical on both the J-

document list and the P-document list. Both list Enoch as a descendant of Adam.

---

19 *And Jared lived after he begat Enoch eight hundred years, and begat sons and daughters:*

20 *And all the days of Jared were nine hundred sixty and two years: and he died.*

21 *And Enoch lived sixty and five years, and begat Methuselah:* [182]

---

182. Methuselah could be the P-document's version of the J-document's Methusael.

---

22 *And Enoch walked with God* [183] *after he begat Methuselah three hundred years, and begat sons and daughters:*

---

183. The phrase "walked with God," or variants thereof, is used in the Bible to mean that a person is pious and lives a virtuous life, fulfilling God's commandments.

---

23 *And all the days of Enoch were three hundred and sixty-five years:* [184]

---

184. Enoch's lifetime of 365 years is very short compared to those of the others named in this chapter, less than half that of any of them, in fact.

The figure 365 gives rise to some speculation that Enoch figured as part of a solar myth; that he may have been a version of a sun-god and had been sanitized by P-document monotheism.

That's only a guess, of course. The Babylonian (and Israelite) year, based on the lunar calendar, was made up of either twelve or thirteen lunar months and might be either 354 or 383 days long (though, on the average, they were 365 days long). Thus, 365 might not have the easy significance to the Biblical writers that it has to us. The number may be a coincidence.

---

24 *And Enoch walked with God: and he was not; for God took him.*[185]

---

185. Whereas of the other people mentioned in this chapter it is said, uniformly, "and he died," for Enoch only is it said "he was not; for God took him." This makes it seem as though the Biblical account would have it that Enoch did *not* die, but was taken alive to Heaven.

The Jews in later times believed so and assumed that in Heaven he learned the workings of the Universe and came to know the future.

In the second century B.C., and thereafter, various books of a mystical nature were written and were said to have been authored by Enoch. These books expanded on various Biblical legends and foretold the manner of the ending of the world.

At least one of those books was sufficiently well known to be mentioned in the New Testament. Thus, in the one-chapter book of Jude, the fourteenth verse reads: "And Enoch also, the seventh from Adam, prophesied of these—" and then quotes from the book in the next two and a half verses.

This notion of having been taken to Heaven alive may be a remnant of sun-god myth or of someone being deified, taken to Heaven, and becoming a sun-god. Enoch, as Jude points out, is the seventh generation, starting with Adam (at least in the P-document). In the list of early Sumerian kings, the seventh is En-men-dur-Anna, who is also described as being the guardian of divine mysteries and as knowing what was to come. What's more, he was king of Sippar, where **Shamash**, the Sume-

143

rian sun-god, was particularly worshipped. However, the writers of the P-document were too careful to remove all traces of polytheism for us to be sure how far the parallelism extends.

---

25 *And Methuselah lived an hundred eighty and seven years, and begat Lamech:* [186]

---

186. Here again we have a name, Lamech, in the P-document list that is identical with one in the J-document list. What's more, Lamech is the son of Methuselah in the P-document list and of Methusael in the J-document list.

---

26 *And Methuselah lived after he begat Lamech seven hundred eighty and two years, and begat sons and daughters:*

27 *And all the days of Methuselah were nine hundred sixty and nine years:* [187] *and he died.*

---

187. Methuselah, having attained the age of 969 years, achieved a record age for any of the people mentioned in the P-document list; and, indeed, for any person mentioned in the Bible. Hence, the well-known phrase, "as old as Methuselah."

---

28 *And Lamech lived an hundred eighty and two years, and begat a son:*

29 *And he called his name Noah,*[188] *saying, This same shall comfort us concerning our work and toil of our hands, because of the ground which the Lord hath cursed.*[189]

---

188. *Noah* is the Hebrew for "rest" or "comfort."

189. This verse, with the use of "Lord" and the reference to the curse that accompanied the expulsion of Adam and Eve from the Garden, is clearly an intrusion of a bit of J-document into a P-document chapter.

Noah is the first person, after Cain and Abel, concerning whom important events are described, so it might have seemed to the Biblical editors that dismissing him in the dry statistical manner of the P-document was insufficient. The J-document verse was added to give some personality to the matter.

If we take the ages at which the various people in the P-document list had their sons and add them up, it turns out that Adam was 874 years old at the time Lamech was born, and he died when Lamech was fifty-six years old. Adam was the first of the people on the list to die—not surprisingly, perhaps. Even Enoch was only 252 years old when Lamech was born, and he outlived Adam by fifty-seven years.

Noah was born 126 years after Adam died and sixty-nine years after Enoch had been taken up to Heaven. Lamech might have felt that with Adam there died the curse that had been placed upon the earth for Adam's sin and that Enoch's piety might have neutralized the sin in any case. Noah, as the first person named in the list to be born after the death of the original sinner and of the pious man, might have been expected to live in a better time.

---

30 *And Lamech lived after he begat Noah five hundred ninety and five years, and begat sons and daughters:*

31 *And all the days of Lamech were seven hundred seventy and seven years:* [190] *and he died.*

---

190. Lamech also had a rather short life by the standards of this chapter. One possible explanation is that

Lamech in the J-document list talked of Cain having been avenged sevenfold while he himself would be avenged seventy-seven fold. It might be that that old song, which was too primitive to be included in the P-document, nevertheless supplied numbers for its numbers-conscious writers.

Lamech died when Noah was 595 years old. Methuselah's stretched-out lifetime meant that he outlived his son, Lamech, by five years and died when Noah was six hundred.

The people mentioned in the Book of Genesis are generally termed "patriarchs" (from Greek words meaning "father-rulers") because so many of them were the ancestral heads of tribes or nations. Because of the extended age of almost all the patriarchs, the word has come to mean any particularly old man. Those who have been mentioned in chapters 2 through 5 of Genesis, having lived before the Flood, are called "antediluvian" ("before the Flood") patriarchs. Hence, the word "antediluvian" has come to mean "very ancient," usually in an unfavorable sense.

---

32 *And Noah was five hundred years old: and Noah begat Shem, Ham, and Japheth.*[191]

---

191. Here the P-document is not as precise as it usually is. It is impossible to tell whether the three sons, Shem, Ham and Japheth, were triplets or whether all three had been born before Noah's five hundredth birthday and were of indeterminate age—at least not from this verse.

It is usually supposed, however, that these three sons were born singly and probably in rapid succession, but at a time when Noah was about five hundred years old. The order in which they are named is taken to signify the order in which they were born, so that Shem is the oldest.

This is the first time in the P-document that a patriarch

is described as having more than one son who is given a name. There is a reason for that.

A catastrophe is soon to come that will destroy all human beings but Noah and his family. That means that all humanity, according to the Biblical tale, must trace its descent from Noah. All human beings who lived before Noah, except for Noah's direct ancestors, have no descendants and are therefore unimportant and need not be named.

The Bible views humanity, however, as being descended from Noah in three large groups, one from each of his sons, since they survived the catastrophe with him. Each of the sons must therefore be named.

Chapter 6

1 *And it came to pass, when men began to multiply on the face of the earth, and daughters were born unto them,*

2 *That the sons of God* [192] *saw the daughters of men that they were fair; and they took them wives of all which they chose.*

192. There now follows an eight-verse portion of the J-document that carries its own story past the song of Lamech and describes the steadily increasing moral corruption of the world.

The passage seems to describe forbidden unions that indicate unbridled sexuality and vice, but it is not clear where the fault lay. The expression "sons of God" seems to refer to divine beings. The impression one gets is that God presided over a divine court filled with godlike beings inferior to himself. This is polytheism, of course, with God merely the chief God of innumerable others.

Because this relic of polytheism in the early legends was inadmissible to later commentators, it was suggested that the "sons of God" were the males of the line of Seth (or possibly men of the upper classes) and the "daughters of men" were the females of the line of Cain (or women of the lower classes), but neither seems likely. In the Book of Job, we see, "Now there was a day when the sons of God came to present themselves before the Lord . . ." (Job 1:6), and there the phrase is clearly used to describe divine beings such as angels. There is no dispute about that.

If the sons of God were divine and enforced their will on helpless human women, would Earth have to suffer for that? To avoid that, there are suggestions by some commentators that the "daughters of men," by means of their lascivious wiles and in order to satisfy their wicked sexual cravings, deliberately seduced the virtuous sons of God. (The real trouble, probably, is that the Biblical editors used an inappropriate portion of the J-document in their effort to find something that would justify the Flood.)

---

3 *And the Lord said, My spirit shall not always strive with man, for that he also is flesh:* [193] *yet his days shall be an hundred and twenty years.* [194]

---

193. This is not clear in the King James. The Revised Standard Version has it read, "My spirit shall not abide in man for ever, for he is flesh."

Perhaps God is reminding himself that man is mortal and that individual sinners have only a limited time in which to weary him with their corruption. Perhaps he is finding excuses for human beings. They are only flesh and therefore weak and bound to sin. The casing of flesh is an imperfect receptacle for the holy spirit.

194. If the interpretation of the first part of the verse is God's self-reminder that man is mortal, then the remainder of the verse is a punishment for human corruption. The mortality of man is emphasized.

Whereas hitherto, individual sinners might weary God with their corruption for nearly a thousand years, now human beings would be confined to a life-span of merely an eighth of that, and would live no more than 120 years. And, as a matter of fact, from this point on, the reported life-spans of the patriarchs after Noah begin to shrink.

As it happens, the maximum life-span of human beings is (as I said earlier) not far short of 120 years.

On the other hand, the more usual interpretation of the verse is not one of punishment but of mercy, in line with the thought that in the first part of the verse, God is finding excuses for humanity. The verse is interpreted to mean that God will withhold punishment for another 120 years, just in case there is repentance and human beings change their ways.

---

4 There were giants in the earth in those days; [195] and also after that, when the sons of God came in unto the daughters of men, and they bare children to them, the same became mighty men which were of old, men of renown.[196]

---

195. The Hebrew word, here translated as "giants" in the King James, is *Nephilim*. There is no clear reason to think that giants is what is meant or that huge physical size is a necessary characteristic. The word is thought to refer to mighty warriors, or to what the Greeks called "heroes," without particular reference to unusual size. The Revised Standard Version evades the issue by leaving the Hebrew word untranslated and having the verse read, "The Nephilim were on the earth in those days."

To be sure, in one sense there were indeed giants in the earth "in those days." Long before *Homo sapiens* appeared on the scene, dinosaurs tramped on the Earth seventy and more million years ago. Some weighed as much as ninety tons. After the dinosaurs died out, there were large mammals, the largest (living about twenty million years ago) being the Baluchitherium, which attained a weight of about twenty-two tons. There were flightless birds, such as the Aepyornis of Madagascar, that weighed up to half a ton and that may not have died out till 1650.

Closer to the human family tree, there was Giganto-pithecus, the largest primate that ever lived. It resembled a giant gorilla, nine feet tall (if it were to stand upright) and weighing some six hundred pounds. It became extinct about three million years ago.

All of these giants, however, are modern discoveries. It passes belief that this Biblical verse could be referring to them.

196. It is very common for legends to speak of great men of renown in the past and to view them as heroes of a greater mold than that to be seen among contemporaries. The past always appears in glorious colors. Homer, writing about 800 B.C., keeps disparaging his contemporaries and telling them how much stronger and more heroic their ancestors were.

In many sets of primitive legends, the great men of the past were viewed as the mixed offspring of the gods and human beings.

Achilles was the son of the sea nymph Thetis; Hercules was the son of Zeus; Aeneas was the son of Aphrodite; Romulus was the son of Mars; and so on. This type of belief is mirrored in this verse of the Bible. It is a bit of a familiar hero-tale of the polytheistic past used by the Biblical editors to emphasize the moral corruption of the times.

That these men of renown of the past were viewed as of supernormal size is natural in view of the exaggerated tales of their deeds. Then, too, there was the natural wonder felt by barbarian invaders at the sight of the works of the civilizations they replaced. Thus, when the Dorian Greeks invaded the Peloponnesus, they were struck with astonishment at the thick walls of towns such as Mycenae and Tiryns, which had been strongholds of the defeated Mycenaean civilization. Unable to grasp what cooperation and technology could accomplish, the Dorians decided that the walls could only have been built by giants.

In the same way, the invading Israelites in 1200 B.C.

viewed the elaborate fortifications of the Canaanite cities with awe; they, too, felt they were fighting giants. The spies sent to report on the Canaanites said, "And there we saw the giants . . . and were in our own sight as grasshoppers . . ." (Numbers 13:33). This must be viewed, however, as metaphor and as dramatic exaggeration.

---

5 *And God saw that the wickedness of man was great in the earth, and that every imagination of the thoughts of his heart was only evil continually.*

6 *And it repented* [197] *the Lord that he had made man on the earth, and it grieved him at his heart.*

---

197. The word "repented" makes it sound as though God had decided he had made a mistake. The Revised Standard Version uses the word "sorry" instead, in parallelism with the word "grieved" later in the verse. Even so, it is clear that God was viewing humanity as an experiment that had failed. In later ages, the concept of God grew more grandiose, and he was viewed as omniscient and incapable of making a mistake. The God of the early legends, however, was a little more human than that.

---

7 *And the Lord said, I will destroy man whom I have created from the face of the earth; both man, and beast, and the creeping thing, and the fowls of the air; for it repenteth me that I have made them.* [198]

---

198. Since Earth and all its life forms were made only for the use of humanity, they became useless without humanity and might all be destroyed. God apparently planned to return everything to Chaos and wash out the whole experiment of Cosmos as a blunder.

8 *But Noah found grace in the eyes of the Lord.*[199]

---

199. That the scheme of a return to Chaos was not carried out totally was owing to the fact that one man, Noah, found grace ("favor") in the eyes of God. The experiment was apparently not a *total* failure, so God decided to wipe out only part of it and then start again.

---

9 *These are the generations of Noah:*[200] *Noah was a just man and perfect in his generations, and Noah walked with God.*[201]

---

200. Here we have a new introduction, which might better be translated, "Following is the story of Noah."

The reason for the introduction is that we now switch to the P-document, which carries on the tale from the end of Chapter 5.

In fact, the story of the Flood, which follows, is to be found both in the P-document and the J-document, each telling it characteristically. The P-document is full of numbers and details, while the J-document concentrates on drama.

The Biblical editors, finding the tale in both documents, included both, interweaving the P-document and the J-document in an attempt to tell a single story. Actually, they managed to introduce repetitions and self-contradictions.

201. The same phrase used in the case of Enoch in the previous chapter is used here in connection with Noah.

---

10 *And Noah begat three sons, Shem, Ham, and Japheth.*

11 *The earth also was corrupt before God, and the earth was filled with violence.*

12 *And God looked upon the earth, and, behold, it was corrupt; for all flesh had corrupted his way upon the earth.*

13 *And God said unto Noah, The end of all flesh is come before me; for the earth is filled with violence through them;* [202] *and, behold, I will destroy them with the earth.*[203]

---

202. In three verses, the P-document says three times that the Earth was corrupt and twice that it was filled with violence, but it gives no details. The P-document knows nothing of the miscegenation of the Sons of God and of the *Nephilim*.

It was perhaps in order to supply some definite excuse for God's destruction of Earth that the Biblical editors scoured the J-document for appropriate verses to place before this section of the Bible. They came up with the Sons of God and with the *Nephilim*, which were inappropriate and mystifying but which were, perhaps, the best they could do.

203. It is God's intention, as is soon to be described, to destroy life on Earth by means of a flood. It requires no great effort of imagination to conceive of a flood as a means of destruction.

Sumeria was a flat land between two large rivers. As is true of any large river (we have only to think of our own Missouri and Mississippi), unusual rises will bring about flooding conditions. In a land as flat as Sumeria, it would not take much of a flood to cover large portions of the entire region.

A particularly bad flood would live on in the memory of later generations, and particularly bad floods undoubtedly occurred. In 1929, the English archaeologist Sir Charles Leonard Woolley reported finding water-deposited layers as much as ten feet thick in excavations near the Euphrates, and Sumerian records speak of events as happening "before the Flood" and "since the Flood."

Naturally, a particularly bad flood would destroy records, especially in a primitive situation where writing had, at best, barely come into use. For that reason, events "before the Flood" would quickly take on a legendary and, very likely, highly exaggerated nature. The Sumerians listed kings who reigned for tens of thousands of years before the Flood; they made no such reports of kings who reigned after the Flood. And, of course, this reflected itself in the ages given of the antediluvian patriarchs in the Bible.

The dramatic tale of the Sumerian Flood was included in the epic of Gilgamesh, which must have been popular all over the ancient world and which couldn't help but influence the myths of other nations.

In the Gilgamesh legend, Gilgamesh, searching for immortality, is directed to seek out Ut-Napishtim, who attained immortality and who also survived the Flood. Gilgamesh finds Ut-Napishtim, and the latter tells a tale very much like the tale in the Bible. Thus, Ut-Napishtim is sometimes called the Sumerian Noah. It might be more accurate to call Noah the Biblical Ut-Napishtim.

River floods, like any other natural disaster, do not usually come about through human agency, and in ancient times, their causes were not understood. The Sumerians assigned the event to the whim of the gods. The Biblical writers, adapting the Sumerian tale, could not allow such whimsicality to stand and searched (not entirely successfully) for a way of showing that humanity had brought the disaster on itself.

---

14 *Make thee an ark [204] of gopher wood; [205] rooms shalt thou make in the ark, and shalt pitch it within and without with pitch.*

---

204. The Hebrew word translated here as "ark" is *tevah,* and means a chest or box. The word "ark" is from a Latin term meaning "to enclose."

We might well suppose that the earliest vessels designed to travel on water were rafts or open boats that

could be rowed or moved by poles or even outfitted with
sails. At first, they were all open to the air. The concept
of a ship closed on all sides (to keep out a torrential rain
that would swamp an open boat) would be that of a giant
box. In modern terms, then, the verse would have begun,
"Make thee an enclosed ship. . . ."

205. *Gopher* is an untranslated Hebrew word. We have
no idea what kind of wood is meant by it.

---

15 *And this is the fashion which thou shalt
make it of: The length of the ark shall be
three hundred cubits, the breadth of it fifty
cubits, and the height of it thirty cubits.*[206]

---

206. As usual, the P-document revels in numbers. A
cubit is about eighteen inches long, so the dimensions of
the ark as described are 450 feet by seventy-five feet by
forty-five feet, for a total volume of a little over 1,500,000
cubic feet. Ut-Napishtim's ark, built at the direction of
the Sumerian god, Ea, was a cube 180 feet on each side,
with a total volume of a little over 5,800,000 cubic feet.

Noah's ark was only a little over a quarter as volu-
minous as Ut-Napishtim's, but Noah's more nearly resembled the proportions of a ship.

---

16 *A window* [207] *shalt thou make to the ark,
and in a cubit shalt thou finish it above:
and the door of the ark shalt thou set in
the side thereof: with lower, second, and
third stories shalt thou make it.*[208]

---

207. A single window in a large vessel designed, as we
shall see, to hold many animals seems absurdly insufficient, but both the Revised Standard Version and the
New English Bible substitute the word "roof" for window, emphasizing the enclosed nature of the vessel.

The Hebrew word translated as "window" actually

means "light," so the Anchor Bible translates it as "sky-light," and Rabbinic legend has it that a precious jewel was used which filled the ark with light.

There is no point in being too meticulous about the detail of the ark. Neither the Sumerians nor the Israelites had experience with large ships or oceanic travel, and the design of the ark is the imaginary description of a group of writers who were, essentially, landlubbers.

208. Ut-Napishtim's vessel was more elaborate and had seven decks.

---

17 And, behold, I, even I, do bring a flood of waters upon the earth, to destroy all flesh, wherein is the breath of life, from under heaven; and everything that is in the earth shall die.

18 But with thee will I establish my covenant: [209] and thou shalt come into the ark, thou, and thy sons, and thy wife, and thy sons' wives with thee.

---

209. A covenant is a solemn contract.

---

19 And of every living thing of all flesh, two of every sort [210] shalt thou bring into the ark, to keep them alive with thee; they shall be male and female.[211]

---

210. "Two of every sort" seemed no big deal to the Biblical writers, who probably identified not more than a few hundred different animals altogether. The Greek philosopher Aristotle, a close and intelligent observer, writing about 350 B.C., could list only about five hundred species of animals.

Yet we now know that there are some fifteen thousand species of mammals alone. Naturally, only a fraction of

these are to be found in Biblical lands, and if the Flood were a local phenomenon of the Tigris-Euphrates region (as it undoubtedly was), those would be all that mattered.

God speaks of destroying *all* flesh, however, and in addition to the mammals there are fifteen thousand species of other land vertebrates and an enormous number of species of other land animals. There are at least a million species of insects, with more being discovered every day. There are five hundred different known species of fleas alone.

It would seem that if God's instructions are taken literally, the ark must have contained anywhere from two to four million animals, some four-fifths of them insects.

211. Having one male and one female of each species is no guarantee of survival. The chances of death of animals is so great that, unless there is a strong system of parental care and a great deal of luck, a single set of parents will not suffice to keep a species alive. The chances are better, of course, if there is no predation and if all animals are vegetarians, as they are supposed to be at this epoch of Biblical history.

---

20 *Of fowls after their kind, and of cattle after their kind, of every creeping thing of the earth after his kind, two of every sort shall come unto thee, to keep them alive.*[212]

---

212. No mention is made of any of the sea animals. Presumably they will not be harmed by the Flood. Microscopic creatures were, of course, unknown.

---

21 *And take thou unto thee of all food that is eaten,[213] and thou shalt gather it to thee; and it shall be for food for thee, and for them.*

---

213. The animal world is still presumably vegetarian, in line with the instructions in Genesis 1:29-30. This means that Noah must collect ample quantities of all plants that are eaten by any of the animals, which, if the verses are accepted literally, would mean *all* land plants, of which there are at least a quarter of a million species.

---

22 *Thus did Noah; according to all that God commanded him, so did he.*

Chapter 7

---

1 *And the Lord* [214] *said unto Noah, Come thou and all thy house into the ark;* [215] *for thee have I seen righteous before me in this generation.*

---

214. The last verse of the sixth chapter speaks of "God"; the first verse of the seventh chapter speaks of "Lord." This is a clear indication that we are back in the J-document, now.

215. The J-document continues from where it left off in Genesis 6:8. Noah has found grace in the eyes of the Lord, who therefore invites him and his house into the ark. The J-document doesn't bother with the dimensions of the ark or its facilities. It is simply there.

---

2 *Of every clean beast* [216] *thou shalt take to thee by sevens,* [217] *the male and his female:* [218] *and of beasts that are not clean* [219] *by two,* [220] *the male and his female.*

---

216. In this verse there is the sudden mention of "clean beasts," without definition. A clean beast is one that can be used in sacrifice, such as cattle, sheep, or goats, but the criteria for distinguishing clean beasts from other kinds are not given until the Book of Leviticus later on in the Bible. The J-document apparently assumes the distinction was always known.

217. Although in the P-document Noah is directed to take a single pair of each kind of living creature without distinction, the J-document has him ordered to take seven pairs of each of the clean beasts. This, it would seem, is not intended to ensure their survival with extra care, but is intended to make sure there is an excess so that some could be sacrificed at the conclusion of the Flood.

218. There is an automatic, taken-for-granted male chauvinism in the Bible and, indeed, in the English language. The P-document refers, when it must, to "male and female," with the male always first. The J-document refers to "the male and his female," reducing the female to the status of property. (Would not the phrase "the female and her male" seem unthinkable?)

219. "Beasts that are not clean" are those that cannot be sacrificed, such as swine, horses, camels, and so on. Again, the distinction is made in Leviticus.

220. The phrase "by two" does not mean two pairs, for then it would be translated in the King James as "by twos" in analogy to the earlier "by sevens." It is always taken to mean a single pair, and in the Revised Standard Version, this portion of the verse is translated "and a pair of the animals that are not clean, the male and his mate."

---

3 *Of fowls also of the air by sevens,*[221] *the male and the female; to keep seed alive upon the face of all the earth.*

---

221. The fowls generally must be supplied in seven pairs each, and there is no mention of unclean fowls. It may be that the J-document speaks only of domesticated animals, for all domesticated birds were clean, but some domesticated mammals were unclean. This makes for a much smaller and more realistic task for the ark than the P-document's version of the ark's having to carry two of every single animal in existence.

---

4 For yet seven days and I will cause it to rain upon the earth forty days and forty nights; [222] and every living substance that I have made will I destroy from off the face of the earth.

---

222. The J-document is not concerned with exact numbers, but forty has certain ritualistic value as a good round number. Moses was on Mount Sinai for forty days, and he lived for three times forty years; Elijah was fed by ravens for forty days; Jesus fasted for forty days; and so on.

---

5 And Noah did according unto all that the Lord commanded him.

6 And Noah was six hundred years old [223] when the flood of waters was upon the earth.

---

223. This verse is from the P-document and follows Genesis 5:22. It is typical of the P-document's concern for ages. Besides, it is not till Noah is six hundred years old that Methuselah dies, if one works out the figures given in the fifth chapter of Genesis. If it is not clear that Methuselah was dead, one might wonder why Noah was so callous as to leave his aged grandfather behind.

If one uses the figures in the fifth chapter, by the way, it turns out that Noah was born 1,056 years after the

Creation and that the Flood took place, therefore, 1,656 years after the Creation. Accepting Archbishop Ussher's estimate that the Creation took place in 4004 B.C., the Flood took place in 2348 B.C.

This would be off only by a few centuries. From the Sumerian records, it would seem that the Flood they speak of may have taken place in 2800 B.C. or thereabouts.

---

7 *And Noah went in, and his sons, and his wife, and his sons' wives with him, into the ark, because of the waters of the flood.*

8 *Of clean beasts, and of beasts that are not clean, and of fowls, and of everything that creepeth upon the earth,*

9 *There went in two and two* [224] *unto Noah into the ark, the male and the female, as God had commanded Noah.*

---

224. It is uncertain whether this means a single pair of each, or in some cases seven pairs, one pair at a time. The ambiguity may be the result of a Biblical editor trying to reconcile the two versions.

---

10 *And it came to pass after seven days, that the waters of the flood were upon the earth.*

11 *In the six hundredth year of Noah's life, in the second month, the seventeenth day of the month,* [225] *the same day were all the fountains of the great deep broken up, and the windows of heaven were opened.* [226]

---

225. Verses 7 through 10 are a portion of the J-document describing the entry into the ark (though it may have been revised by the editor, using God instead of

Lord and obscuring the actual numbers of each species).

With verse 11, however, we return to the P-document, and the entry into the ark will be described all over again. The P-document gives not only the year of the entry, but the exact month and day, which is typical of its concern for numbers.

226. There is at least a partial breakdown of the cosmic order as the divisions between land and sea, and between the waters below and above the firmament, are broken down.

If we consider the actual Flood in Sumerian history, does the mention of the "fountains of the great deep" mean that it was more than a river flood? Did the waters of the ocean also invade the land? Were heavy rains accompanied by a great tsunami (or tidal wave) as well?

What might have caused the tsunami? There is a crustal-plate boundary that runs down the northeastern shore of the Persian Gulf, and it is possible that an earthquake may have taken place in such a way as to shake the sea and send a wave of water careening up the Gulf.

More dramatically still, we might speculate that perhaps a sizable meteor made an unlucky strike on the waters of the Gulf and created a huge splash. There is no evidence for either of these speculations, but neither is flatly impossible.

---

12 *And the rain was upon the earth forty days and forty nights.*[227]

---

227. Here is the insertion of a J-document verse in the midst of a P-document passage, referring once again to the forty-day rain of the fourth verse of this chapter.

---

13 *In the selfsame day entered Noah, and Shem, and Ham, and Japheth, the sons of Noah, and Noah's wife, and the three wives of his sons with them, into the ark;*

14 They, and every beast after his kind, and all the cattle after their kind, and every creeping thing that creepeth upon the earth after his kind, and every fowl after his kind, every bird of every sort.

15 And they went in unto Noah into the ark, two and two of all flesh, wherein is the breath of life.

16 And they that went in, went in male and female of all flesh, as God had commanded him: [228] and the Lord shut him in.[229]

---

228. This is the P-document description of the entry into the ark, very much a repetition of the J-document description.

229. The final phrase of this verse is a return to the J-document. It should have come at the end of the J-document description of the entry at the end of verse 9, but its note of finality would have made it a little more difficult to go on with the P-document description of the entry, so it was placed here.

---

17 And the flood was forty days upon the earth; [230] and the waters increased, and bare up the ark, and it was lift up above the earth.

---

230. Again the J-document mentions the forty-day period. This time it is not merely to say that it will rain for forty days, but that the duration of the Flood (presumably the total duration) was forty days.

---

18 And the waters prevailed and were increased greatly upon the earth; and the ark went upon the face of the waters.[231]

---

231. This verse is essentially a repetition of the preceding one, but now it is the P-document that is being quoted, and there is no mention of the forty days.

---

19 *And the waters prevailed exceedingly upon the earth; and all the high hills, that were under the whole heaven, were covered.*[232]

---

232. Assuming that the Flood was, in actual fact, confined to the Tigris-Euphrates valley, it is not surprising that "all the high hills" were covered. The valley is flat, and elevations are not great. In a bad flood or tsunami or both, everything in the region would indeed be covered.

To the stricken survivors, it would certainly seem that all elevations "that were under the whole heaven" were covered. But then the Sumerians of 2800 B.C. could scarcely have had much more than a very local idea of the extent of the world.

If one were to accept the verse literally and assume that the Flood covered the entire world as we know it today (as, in fact, most Biblical readers did assume, and probably still do assume today), then we would have to imagine that the sea level rose five and a half miles in order to cover even the Himalayas. The amount of water required to raise the sea level by that amount is over three and a half times the total quantity of water on Earth.

---

20 *Fifteen cubits upward did the waters prevail: and the mountains were covered.*[233]

---

233. Fifteen cubits is about twenty-two feet, and this is laughably insufficient to cover the mountains, or even low hills, if we accept the implication of the verse as given in the King James Version: that the water was

twenty-two feet deep and that this was sufficient to cover the mountains.

A more correct interpretation, perhaps, given in the Revised Standard Version, reads, "the waters prevailed above the mountains, covering them fifteen cubits deep."

In other words, the total depth of the water was twenty-two feet higher than Mt. Everest's 29,028 feet, so that the sea level at the height of the Flood was 29,050 feet (5.5 miles) above the present sea level.

From the scientific standpoint, this is clearly impossible, since there is not enough water on Earth to accomplish the task; what is more, there is no sign of such a universal deluge in the third millennium B.C. Egyptian history, for instance, carries right through the entire third millennium B.C. without any sign of a break or any mention of a flood.

On the other hand, if we consider the flatness of the Tigris-Euphrates valley, and consider the Flood to have been a local phenomenon of the region, we might well imagine twenty-two feet to be a sober estimate of the depth to which the elevations of the region were covered.

---

21 *And all flesh died that moved upon the earth, both of fowl, and of cattle, and of beast, and of every creeping thing that creepeth upon the earth, and every man:*

22 *All in whose nostrils was the breath of life, of all that was in the dry land* [234] *died.*

---

234. The implication is that sea life was not disturbed.

It is a horrible death by drowning that is thus unemotionally dismissed in the Bible. One can imagine drenched people trying to find high ground, trying to keep their heads above water. We can imagine animals fleeing uselessly. Whatever their sins, a more merciful deity, one might imagine, would have simply swept them painlessly out of existence with a word, and begun over again.

23 *And every living substance was destroyed which was upon the face of the ground, both man, and cattle, and the creeping things, and the fowl of the heaven; and they were destroyed from the earth: and Noah only remained alive, and they that were with him in the ark.*[235]

235. In three successive verses, it is stated that every living thing on the dry land died. This needless repetition arises from the fact that verse 21 is the J-document saying so, while verses 22 and 23 are the P-document saying so, and the Biblical editors decided that both statements must be included.

24 *And the waters prevailed upon the earth an hundred and fifty days.*[236]

236. The J-document has the rains lasting for forty days and forty nights, but the P-document has the waters "prevailing" for 150 days. In order to avoid any contradiction, some commentators assume that it rained for forty days, bringing the flood to its crest, and that the crest was maintained, without additional rain, for 150 additional days (or perhaps for a total of 150 days, counting the forty days of rain).

It makes more sense to suppose that the two documents tell stories that differ from each other in various ways.

Chapter 8

1 *And God remembered Noah, and every living thing, and all the cattle that was with him in the ark: and God made a wind to pass over the earth,[237] and the waters assuaged.*

237. This wind is presumably the breath or "Spirit of God," which in Genesis 1:2 began the task of creating Order out of Chaos. Now that Chaos has in part returned, the Spirit must refurbish Order.

2 *The fountains also of the deep and the windows of heaven were stopped,[238] and the rain from heaven was restrained;[239]*

238. This, following the previous two verses, all of which is from the P-document, makes it clear that the rain had continued for 150 days, according to the P-document, and that Order had been flowing back to Chaos for that period—until the Spirit of God intervened.

239. Stating that "the rain from heaven was restrained" repeats that "the windows of heaven were stopped." The repetition arises from the apparent fact that the earlier phrase is part of the P-document and the later part of the J-document. It is only in the P-document that mention is made of the fountains of the deep and the windows of heaven, implying a return to Chaos and a reversal of the deeds of Genesis 1. In the J-document, only rain is mentioned.

3 *And the waters returned from off the earth continually:[240] and after the end of the hundred and fifty days the waters were abated.[241]*

240. This first part of the verse is from the J-document and presumably describes the waters draining away after the rain of forty days and forty nights.

241. This second part of the verse is from the P-document, and it states that the waters began to drain away after 150 days, mentioning the time specifically.

---

4 *And the ark rested in the seventh month, on the seventeenth day of the month,[242] upon the mountains of Ararat.[243]*

---

242. The rains started on the seventeenth day of the second month, so that exactly five lunar months had passed at the time the "ark rested." That is just about 147.5 days—roughly, 150 days.

243. At the time the Flood reached its crest, then, by the reckoning of the P-document, the ark was in Ararat. This is a mountainous kingdom where the Tigris and Euphrates both have their sources in what is now eastern Turkey. It flourished in Assyrian times, and its name was Urartu—of which Ararat is clearly a version.

The tradition that the ark came to rest among the mountain ranges of Urartu is rather a point in favor of the tsunami theory of the Flood. Ordinary river flooding would sweep floating objects downstream—southeastward into the Persian Gulf. A huge tsunami would sweep it upstream—northwestward toward Urartu.

Despite the fact that a land is named, and a mountain range, there is a general feeling that Ararat is the name of a definite mountain peak. Indeed, the name was eventually applied to one. Mount Ararat is found on modern maps in the easternmost region of Turkey, about seventy miles northeast of Lake Van. Its highest peak is 16,783 feet (3.2 miles) above sea level.

There are fanciful tales now and then of mysterious wooden objects located on its upper slopes, but none of these tales will withstand serious scrutiny.

5 *And the waters decreased continually un-*
til the tenth month: in the tenth month, on
the first day of the month,[244] *were the tops*
of the mountains seen.[245]

244. This would be 218 days after the beginning of the Flood and sixty-eight days after the waters began to recede.

245. In the preceding verse, it is stated that the "ark rested . . . upon the mountains of Ararat." If this is taken to mean that the ark came to rest on a mountain peak, why would this verse say that it took sixty-eight days of recession before the mountain peaks were visible above the water?

It might be better to suppose that the ark floated to Urartu and then floated no more, but came to rest there, and when the mountain peaks were exposed, it reached land on one of them.

6 *And it came to pass at the end of forty*
days, that Noah opened the window of the
ark which he had made: [246]

246. This makes it seem as though Noah waited for forty days after the mountain peaks appeared above the waters. However, we are back in the J-document now, and in that version of the story, it would appear that there was a rain of forty days and nights, followed by a reasonably rapid recession of waters. In this version of the story, apparently, Noah begins to investigate the situation at the instant the rains ceased.

7 *And he sent forth a raven, which went*
forth to and fro,[247] *until the waters were*
dried up from off the earth.

247. In this portion of the J-document Flood-story, there is a similarity to the Sumerian Flood-story. Ut-Napishtim sends out three birds—a dove, a raven, and a swallow—to act as reconnaissance. Noah's raven, as described in this verse, seems to serve no purpose.

---

8 *Also he sent forth a dove from him to see if the waters were abated from off the face of the ground.*

9 *But the dove found no rest for the sole of her foot, and she returned unto him into the ark, for the waters were on the face of the whole earth:* [248] *then he put forth his hand, and took her, and pulled her in unto him into the ark.*

---

248. The dove, which Noah sends out as a second bird, *does* perform an effective reconnaissance function. The only reason for mentioning the raven at all would be to tie in with the Sumerian Flood-story, one might think.

If the dove could find no resting place because the waters were on the face of the whole earth, she must indeed have reconnoitered far and wide. Here again is an indication that the Flood was a local phenomenon and that the Sumerian knowledge of the world at the time of the Flood was restricted indeed.

---

10 *And he stayed yet other seven days; and again he sent forth the dove out of the ark;*

11 *And the dove came in to him in the evening; and lo, in her mouth was an olive leaf* [249] *pluckt off: so Noah knew that the waters were abated from off the earth.* [250]

---

249. The olive is an old symbol of peace. Olive trees

170

require careful cultivation for years before they begin to bear their much desired fruit, so that a flourishing olive grove is an indication that the region has known peace. Had there been an invading army, it would have been sure to hack down the olive trees in order to impoverish and weaken the enemy for a number of years.

Similarly, the dove is a symbol of peace because it is a gentle bird that makes soft, cooing noises.

Primarily because of this particular verse in the Bible, the double symbol—a dove carrying an olive branch (though the Bible says merely "leaf")—is the accepted symbol for peace among us.

250. The land has been under water forty-seven days, according to the J-document; at least three hundred days, according to the P-document; but an olive tree is still alive.

Actually, land plants covered by a deep layer of ocean water for an extended period will die just as surely as land animals will. The Biblical writers, however, did not view plants as living things, but merely as an outgrowth of the Earth. It would seem natural to them that once the dry land was exposed again, its outgrowth would form at once—or perhaps had never disappeared.

---

12 *And he stayed yet other seven days; and sent forth the dove; which returned not again unto him any more.*[251]

---

251. We might be concerned that the dove's mate might not find him (or her, for the Bible does not specify the sex of this dove) and that the survival of the dove was placed in jeopardy.

The tale of the raven and the dove is part of the J-document Flood-story, however, and in the J-document, there were seven pairs of the clean animals taken. Since the dove is a clean animal, there were some to spare for survival.

13 And it came to pass in the six hundred and first year,[252] in the first month, the first day of the month,[253] the waters were dried up from off the earth: and Noah removed the covering of the ark, and looked, and, behold, the face of the ground was dry.

252. We are back in the P-document, with its concern for time. The 601st year refers to Noah's age.

253. This is 337 days after the start of the Flood, by the chronology of the P-document.

14 And in the second month, on the seven and twentieth day of the month, was the earth dried.[254]

254. In two successive verses, the earth is declared as dry; first at the beginning of the year, then nearly three months later. Both statements are in the P-document.

The usual explanation is that at the beginning of the year, the ground was totally exposed but still marshy and muddy. It was not till nearly three months later that the earth was completely dry, as it had been before the Flood.

If this interpretation is accepted, then the total duration of the Flood from the seventeenth day of the second month of the 600th year to the twenty-seventh day of the second month of the 601st year is twelve lunar months and eleven days, or 365 days. This is exactly one solar year.

15 And God spake unto Noah, saying,

16 Go forth of the ark, thou, and thy wife, and thy sons, and thy sons' wives with thee.

17 Bring forth with thee every living thing that is with thee, of all flesh, both of fowl, and of cattle, and of every creeping thing that creepeth upon the earth; that they may breed abundantly in the earth, and be fruitful, and multiply upon the earth.

18 And Noah went forth, and his sons, and his wife, and his sons' wives with him:

19 Every beast, every creeping thing, and every fowl and whatsoever creepeth upon the earth, after their kinds, went forth out of the ark.

20 And Noah builded an altar unto the Lord; and took of every clean beast, and of every clean fowl, and offered burnt offerings on the altar.[255]

---

255. This verse switches to the J-document, and it is because of this sacrifice that the J-document describes seven pairs of each clean animal as having been in the ark. The P-document, without the sacrifice, needs only one pair of each animal, clean or unclean.

---

21 And the Lord smelled a sweet savour: [256] and the Lord said in his heart, I will not again curse the ground any more for man's sake; for the imagination of man's heart is evil from his youth; neither will I again smite any more every thing living, as I have done.

---

256. In the Sumerian Flood-story, Ut-Napishtim also sacrifices to the gods, who flock gratefully about the smoke, gathering "like flies." The impression one gets is that the gods have been starved for the smell of the sacrifices, which is their food, and they are grateful for the renewal. Enlil, the Sumerian god of the earth who, out of

enmity for humanity, sent the Flood, is enraged that any life escaped. The other gods, however, led by Ea (god of fresh water, who, as a friend of human beings, warned Ut-Napishtim of the coming of the Flood), managed to assuage Enlil's anger and appease him. They labored to do so, presumably, because they dreaded starvation, and even Enlil decided he would rather let human beings live than do without the smell of sacrifices.

The Bible tones this down a good deal, but the Lord "smelled a sweet savour" and at once decided to lift the curse on the ground, placed in Adam's day, and to devastate Earth no more.

---

22 *While the earth remaineth,*[257] *seedtime and harvest, and cold and heat, and summer and winter, and day and night shall not cease.*[258]

---

257. The phrase "while the earth remaineth" might be taken to imply that the earth is not necessarily eternal. If it were, it would have been sufficient for the verse to read, "Seedtime and harvest, and cold and heat, and summer and winter, and day and night shall not cease."

The Biblical view (taking the Bible as a whole) is that the Earth—in its present form, at least—will someday end. The Book of Revelation described the process in graphic detail.

From the scientific point of view, too, Earth is not necessarily eternal. There are a variety of catastrophes that could conceivably damage it badly enough to make human life upon it impossible, though most of these are very low-probability events. Even if Earth escapes such catastrophes, however, then by some seven billion years hence the sun will have consumed enough of its hydrogen fuel to enter the next stage of its evolution.

It will be expanding, little by little, into a red giant. Its surface will then be considerably cooler than it is now, but the amount of surface will increase so enormously that it will deliver much more heat in total. Besides, as

174

the sun expands, that surface will come nearer to Earth and may even engulf it.

It is quite certain that as the sun expands, life on Earth will become impossible, and at the height of the expansion, the solid body of our planet may even vaporize.

258. Even though Earth continues to exist, it may well be that the orderly cycle of nature could be interrupted despite this promise that Earth's rotation about its axis (day and night) and its revolution about the sun (seedtime and harvest, cold and heat, summer and winter) shall continue uninterrupted and unmodified.

In the scientific description of Earth's past, it turns out that the planet has gone through drastic ice ages. In those periods, huge ice sheets weighed down the more polar reaches of the continents; the sea level dropped three hundred feet because much water was tied up as ice on land; the weather pattern of the planet changed tremendously.

Past ice ages have not seriously interfered with life on Earth because both the coming and going of the ice has been very slow. Besides, new land exposed at the rim of the continents through the lowering of the sea level made up for the land buried under the ice. Finally, sea life was untouched by the ice age; if anything, it was helped since the slightly lower average temperature of the ocean allowed more oxygen to be dissolved in it.

Until now, however, the ice ages that humanity and its hominid precursors have experienced have come at a time when they were food-gatherers. During the next ice age (and another one may be inevitable, sooner or later) there are likely to be far more people on Earth than in the past, and these people would be far more firmly fixed in place by cities, farms, mines, and so on.

Humanity may nevertheless survive and, in fact, probably will, but the smooth succession of seasons promised in this verse will have failed.

Chapter 9

1 *And God blessed Noah and his sons, and said unto them, Be fruitful, and multiply, and replenish the earth,*

2 *And the fear of you and the dread of you shall be upon every beast of the earth, and upon every fowl of the air, upon all that moveth upon the earth, and upon all the fishes of the sea; into your hand are they delivered.*[259]

259. A new start must be made, so God repeats the blessing he had originally bestowed on the first human beings he had created in Genesis 1:28.

3 *Every moving thing that liveth shall be meat for you;* [260] *even as the green herb have I given you all things.*

260. Human beings (and presumably other animals) are now, for the first time, allowed to be carnivorous. (From the scientific viewpoint, of course, human beings have been carnivorous from the time they first evolved, and carnivorousness in general is as old as life, perhaps.)

This is the P-document, and no distinction is made here between clean and unclean (as it is in the J-document). "Every moving thing that liveth" it is permissible to eat.

4 *But flesh with the life thereof, which is the blood thereof,*[261] *shall ye not eat.*

261. It is tempting to think that breath is the principle of life. Hence the comparison of God with breath in Gen-

esis 1:2 and 8:1, and Adam's receiving life by way of breath.

It is also tempting to think that blood is the principle of life. We still speak of "flesh and blood." We no longer have the feeling of the significance of that phrase, but flesh represents the material housing of the life-force, itself inanimate, and blood *is* the life-force.

After all, blood is pumped to every part of the body by the heart, and even if the ancients did not have the concept of the circulation of the blood, they did know that blood was in every part of the body and that the heart continued beating throughout life—and was stilled in death. They also knew that death ensued if enough blood escaped from the body.

Science does not dispute the overwhelming importance of either breath or blood to the life of human beings and other animals. There is no chance, however, that life is so simple a phenomenon as to rest in either or both of these entities. Each merely contributes its part to a much more complex whole. Science pursues life down to the molecular level and finds it resting on very complex molecules in very complex interrelationships.

It is because plants do not seem to breathe and do not possess blood that it was easy for the Biblical writers to assume that they were not alive but were merely outgrowths of the soil. In actual fact, plants *do* breathe, but less noticeably than animals do. And if they lack blood, they nevertheless possess a circulating sap, which performs certain vital functions analogous to those of blood.

---

5 *And surely your blood of your lives will I require; at the hand of every beast will I require it, and at the hand of man; at the hand of every man's brother will I require the life of man.*

6 *Whoso sheddeth man's blood by man shall his blood be shed: for in the image of God made he man.* [262]

---

262. This is the first divine prohibition since Adam was

forbidden to eat the fruit of the tree of knowledge. Murder is now forbidden. The rationale seems to be that blood (life) is the gift of God and therefore cannot be taken away but by God.

If a human being (or a beast, for that matter, as the preceding verse specifies) "sheddeth man's blood," blasphemy has been committed, for a gift of God has been stolen. The murderer's act has forfeited his own gift of life, and he can then be freely killed without the killer incurring the penalties of blasphemy.

This marks the situation in many societies that are preliterate and that have no fixed written laws. When a person is killed, the members of the group to which that person belonged feel the right, and even duty, to even the score by killing the killer or some member of the killer's group. (This is the danger Cain feared in Genesis 4:14.) If the killer's tribe feels the score has been more than evened, it seeks to redress the balance in turn, and the result is a "blood feud" that may end in dozens of killings.

The unsatisfactory nature of this blood feud is such that even in preliterate societies attempts would be made to bring it under control, while in any literate society with a written code of laws, the crime of murder must be considered by a judge according to certain legal forms and a punishment must be established in accordance with the gravity of offense—and that punishment must end the matter.

Nor need the punishment always be death—since there can be such things as accidental homicide, homicide in a moment of passion, homicide in self-defense, and so on. There are no gradations recognized in this Biblical verse, and for this reason, too, it marks a very primitive stage in human development.

This verse has been used to justify capital punishment, and it also gives rise to the feeling that murder isn't really so bad or as culpable if no blood is shed in the process. Thus Odo, Bishop of Bayeux, a half-brother of William the Conqueror, went into battle with a mace. Killing an enemy by brain concussion seemed more godly than to make use of swords, spears, and arrows, weapons designed to draw blood.

7 And you, be ye fruitful, and multiply;
bring forth abundantly in the earth, and
multiply therein.

8 And God spake unto Noah, and to his sons
with him,[263] saying,

263. In the J-document, the Lord's determination not to
destroy his handiwork a second time is a matter of silent
decision (see Genesis 8:21). Here, in the P-document, God
expresses the determination directly to Noah and his
sons. The P-document tends to be legalistic, and a contract ("covenant") is about to be set up.

9 And I, behold, I establish my covenant
with you, and with your seed after you; [264]

264. In a way, forbidding the eating of the fruit of the
tree of knowledge was a contract. Adam agreed not to
eat the fruit, and in return God would not allow death to
enter the world. By eating it, Adam broke the contract.

Now the contract is restated in a more positive way.
Noah and his sons are to obey the injunctions against
murder and the eating of blood, and God would not
again destroy the world but would allow life to continue.

10 And with every living creature that is with
you, of the fowl, of the cattle, and of every
beast of the earth with you; from all that
go out of the ark, to every beast of the
earth.[265]

265. This sounds as though God contracts to preserve
every species, and to be sure, men have in the past felt
that all species not only existed from the beginning but
would continue to exist to the end. We now know, how-

ever, that many species have become extinct and many species are becoming extinct each year—usually through human action.

---

11 *And I will establish my covenant with you; neither shall all flesh be cut off any more by the waters of a flood;* [266] *neither shall there any more be a flood to destroy the earth.*[267]

---

266. Since it is quite obvious that the edicts against murder and against eating blood have never been generally observed by human beings, we can only assume that after Noah's time, God would content himself with punishing the sinner only and not "all flesh" generally as before. Furthermore, the punishment would not be by the agency of a flood, although, presumably, other methods would remain available to God.

267. From the scientific view, the promise of no further flood cannot fail, for there is not enough water on Earth to make such a flood possible either in Noah's time or since.

If, however, we assume the meaning of "earth" to the Sumerians—as representing a river valley and immediately neighboring territory—then the promise has not been kept. There have been innumerable flooding disasters in the last four thousand years, some of which drowned more people than the Sumerian flood of 2800 B.C. or thereabouts is likely to have done. Every year, in fact, sees flooding somewhere.

---

12 *And God said, This is the token of the covenant* [268] *which I make between me and you and every living creature that is with you, for perpetual generations:*

---

268. In order for a contract to be legally binding, there must be witnesses to the actual agreement, and God provides one in the form of an atmospheric phenomenon.

---

13 *I do set my bow in the cloud,*[269] *and it shall be for a token of a covenant between me and the earth.*

---

269. The "bow" is the rainbow. The verse might be interpreted to mean that God, having reduced the Universe at least partway to chaos in the course of the Flood, now has the chance to put in afterthoughts and creates the rainbow, which had not previously existed. On the other hand, in view of the fact that the P-document Creation-story states the Universe to have been "finished," one might alternatively suppose that the rainbow had existed before the Flood but was now bent to a new use.

The rainbow always strikes people with awe and astonishment, and between its position and its shape, it was easy to imagine it to be a bridge over which there could be communication between heaven and earth. In the Greek myths, Iris, the messenger of the gods, reaches Earth by way of the rainbow. Indeed "iris" means "rainbow." In the Norse myths, the rainbow is also the bridge whereby the gods come down to Earth, and on the evening of the final battle between the gods and the forces of evil, the rainbow bridge breaks under the thundering hooves of the heroes of Valhalla.

In actual fact, we have learned from scientific investigation that the rainbow is a spectrum, a division of white light (which is a mixture of tiny waves of different lengths) into progression of increasing wavelength, from the shortest, which impress the brain as violet light, to the longest, which impress it as red light. The rainbow can be duplicated by triangular blocks of glass called prisms or by other devices. After a rain, there are still tiny droplets suspended in the air, and each of these acts as a tiny refracting device. All together produce the rainbow, which requires only the sun, air, and water droplets to exist—and which undoubtedly existed for billions of years before human beings evolved.

---

14 *And it shall come to pass, when I bring a cloud over the earth, that the bow shall be seen in the cloud:*

15 *And I will remember my covenant, which is between me and you and every living creature of all flesh; and the waters shall no more become a flood to destroy all flesh.*

16 *And the bow shall be in the cloud; and I will look upon it, that I may remember the everlasting covenant between God and every living creature of all flesh that is upon the earth.*

17 *And God said unto Noah, This is the token of the covenant, which I have established between me and all flesh that is upon the earth.*[270]

---

270. This is a rather repetitious passage. It is almost as though God, having once before urged the animal world (including man) to be fruitful and multiply and replenish the earth, and having then negated the blessing in the form of a universal Flood, is now anxious to assure life that this time he means it—and therefore he repeats it several times.

---

18 *And the sons of Noah, that went forth of the ark, were Shem, and Ham, and Japheth: and Ham is the father of Canaan.*[271]

---

271. The J-document takes up the story here, and the

182

reference to Canaan would seem, at this point, to be a non sequitur and unnecessary.

The Biblical writers, however, are chiefly interested in the history of the Israelites, and the Israelites lived in the land of Canaan by right of conquest.

Because the Bible uses a theological approach to history, all events are interpreted as in accord with the will of God and as being based on justice. Good fortune is the result of obedience to divine law; bad fortune to disobedience. If the land of Canaan has been conquered, and if the people who had earlier dwelt there were enslaved by the Israelites, this had to be described as the just consequence of some evil done by the Canaanites or by some ancestor.

Canaan, the son of Ham and grandson of Noah, is the eponymous ancestor of the Canaanites, and since an event is about to be told that will serve as the explanation for the enslavement of the Canaanites, Canaan is brought into the tale.

---

19 *These are the three sons of Noah: and of them was the whole earth overspread.*[272]

---

272. It would be as naive to take the phrase "the whole earth" literally here as it would be in the story of the Flood.

The details that follow will make it clear that the Biblical writers are discussing only parts of what we now call the Middle East—the regions they knew. There is no indication of any knowledge of the Americas or Australia or distant islands; not even any knowledge of the farther reaches of Europe, Asia, and Africa.

Even in a more restricted sense, there is no indication of any possibility that the Sumerian Flood reduced even the Middle East to a single family. Areas such as Egypt, Asia Minor, Crete, and so on were well populated both before and after the traditional time of the Flood, with no detectable signs of any catastrophic break whatever.

20 *And Noah began to be an husbandman,*
and he planted a vineyard: [273]

---

273. It is usually supposed that this verse indicates Noah to have been the first to cultivate grapes. Actually, the cultivation of grapevines is much older than the supposed time of Noah, just as farming is much older than the supposed time of Cain. Egyptian records dating back to 2400 B.C. (just about the supposed time of the Flood, as indicated by Biblical chronology) already refer to grape-growing as an ancient and well-developed form of human endeavor.

---

21 *And he drank of the wine, and was*
drunken; [274] *and he was uncovered within*
his tent.[275]

---

274. It is usually supposed that Noah, ignorant of the effects of wine and pleased with the taste, drank more than was good for him. This may well have been the way in which the effects of alcohol were discovered in prehistoric times.

275. Fruit ferments naturally under certain conditions. When eaten, such fruits produce effects that are sometimes found desirable. The loss of the usual sober relation to the surrounding world may be interpreted as a way of getting through to a supernatural and divine world. Fermented fruits may then have been sought out, ways of deliberately encouraging the fermentation may have been worked out, and religious festivals organized that centered about the drinking of wine. (The Greek worship of Dionysus is an example.)

A modern example involves the synthetic substance lysergic acid diethylamide, better known as LSD. Its hallucinogenic nature was discovered by a chemist quite by accident. It wasn't long, though, before the hallucinogenic character was exploited by people who found significance and value in disordering their mind in this fashion and invested the process with a quasi-religious function.

It is conceivable that this verse is all that is left of an earlier legend that had Noah engaging in some Dionysiac revelry; something that was toned down considerably by the shocked prudery of the Biblical writers.

---

22 *And Ham, the father of Canaan* [276]*, saw the nakedness of his father,*[277] *and told his two brethren without.*[278]

---

276. Again Canaan is mentioned. Some speculate that the villain of the story is not really Ham, but Canaan. In that case, it is hard to see why the Biblical writers should not say so. It would be to their interest to make Canaan as villainous as possible.

277. The expression "saw the nakedness of his father" may well be a euphemistic expression to represent something much worse than merely witnessing (perhaps accidentally) a naked father in a drunken stupor. Perhaps Ham witnessed his father's Dionysiac revelry and joined him or, worse, encouraged him.

278. Whatever it was Ham did, the implication was that he found it amusing and told Shem and Japheth, presumably expecting them to share in the mirth. It is not hard to see that this is a matter of adding insult to injury and that it compounds the offense.

---

23 *And Shem and Japheth took a garment, and laid it upon both their shoulders, and went backward, and covered the nakedness of their father; and their faces were backward, and they saw not their father's nakedness.*

24 *And Noah awoke from his wine, and knew what his younger son*[279] *had done unto him.*[280]

---

279. Since Shem, Ham, and Japheth are mentioned in that order every time, it is commonly assumed that Ham is the second son and, therefore, a "younger son." However, the Hebrew words used in this place mean "youngest son," and they are so translated in the Revised Standard Version, for instance.

This could be a copyist's mistake in early times, one that has been faithfully reproduced ever since. Some suggest that "youngest son" means here "grandson" and that it is Canaan that is referred to. Again, as is described later, Ham had four sons, with Canaan the youngest, so the whole story may not be about Noah and Ham, but about Ham and Canaan. It is hopeless, however, to try to penetrate the confusion on the basis of the Biblical verses alone.

280. The phrase "done unto him" may refer simply to Ham (or Canaan) having seen Noah's shameful state and having joked about it.

There is, however, some speculation that something more, and worse, could be involved. In the Book of Leviticus, the phrase "to uncover the nakedness" is a euphemism for sexual relations. Thus we have: "None of you shall approach to any that is near of kin to him, to uncover their nakedness: I am the Lord./ The nakedness of thy father, or the nakedness of thy mother, shalt thou not uncover: she is thy mother; thou shalt not uncover her nakedness" (Leviticus 18:6-7). These and the following verses forbid incest.

Might Ham (or Canaan) have taken advantage of Noah's drunkenness to commit some sexual act? Some even speculate that what took place was not incest but castration.

There are castration legends in myths. The best known is in the Greek myths, where Kronos castrated his father

Ouranos and took over the rule of the Universe. (Castration, after all, would mean the ruler is no longer a functioning male, and that might well disqualify him from further occupying his post. Then, too, it would prevent the ruler from giving birth to more children who might later dispute the inheritance.)

Could it be that Ham (or Canaan) castrated Noah in an attempt to rule the world (still relatively unpeopled in the wake of the Flood), but that Shem and Japheth, in alliance, prevented it? That is all purely speculation, however, and the literal reading of the Bible does not support a greater crime for Ham than accidental voyeurism.

---

25 *And he said, Cursed be Canaan;* [281] *a servant of servants shall he be unto his brethren.*

---

281. Again, this may be an indication that the original version of the legend implicated Canaan rather than Ham. Or it may be that the Biblical writers were anxious to implicate Canaan for their own purposes.

There have been some who have considered Ham to have been a black and who have used the curse to justify black slavery. Even if such an argument were permissible, it is soon apparent that Ham was *not* a black. In the next chapter, the descendants of Ham are described, and it is clear they are ancient peoples who are well known and who were not blacks.

---

26 *And he said, Blessed be the Lord God of Shem; and Canaan shall be his servant.*

27 *God shall enlarge Japheth, and he shall dwell in the tents of Shem;* [282] *and Canaan shall be his servant.*

---

282. No one has been able to explain this verse or to point out the clear significance of Japheth dwelling in the tents of Shem. Something may have been left out or distorted in the copying, and it may then be hopeless to puzzle out the meaning.

---

28 *And Noah lived after the flood three hundred and fifty years.*

29 *And all the days of Noah were nine hundred and fifty years:* [283] *and he died.*

---

283. Noah is the last person in the Bible who is stated to have lived to be over nine hundred years. There were seven of them altogether: Adam, Seth, Enos, Cainan, Jared, Methuselah, and Noah. From here on, the ages upon death, as they are given, decrease little by little until the present normal life-span is reached.

At that, the P-document again errs on the side of caution. After all, Ut-Napishtim is granted immortality after the flood by the gods. Noah is not. He doesn't even live as long as his grandfather Methuselah.

Chapter 10

---

1 *Now these are the generations of the sons of Noah, Shem, Ham and Japheth:* [284] *and unto them were sons born after the flood.*

---

284. After this second creation, the Biblical writers quickly organized the nations of the world, or of that part of it known to them, so that they could then proceed to concern themselves with the Israelites, who served as the central theme of their world story.

The three sons of Noah represent the three great divisions of the peoples known to the ancient writers of the Bible.

In general, the descendants of Shem are pictured as occupying the Arabian peninsula and the regions adjoining it to the north, including the Tigris-Euphrates regions. Since the descendants include the Israelites themselves, Shem is given the post of honor and is made the eldest son of Noah.

The languages of these descendants are referred to, in modern times, as "Semitic" ("Sem" is the Graeco-Latin form of Shem). These languages include Hebrew, Assyrian, Aramaean, and Arabic.

The descendants of Ham are described as inhabiting chiefly the corner of Africa adjacent to Asia. For this reason, the original languages of the area are called "Hamitic." This includes Coptic, the Berber languages of North Africa, and some of the languages of Ethiopia, such as Amharic.

The descendants of Japheth are described as inhabiting the regions to the north and east of the Tigris-Euphrates. Sometimes "Japhetic" is used to refer to certain languages in the Caucasus region. The term "Indo-European" is usually used, however, since related languages cover a broad swath from Spain to India.

The writers of Genesis were not influenced by language, however. Modern notions of philology are strictly modern. Rather, the Biblical writers were guided by political connections and by geographic propinquity. Such connections often did bespeak common ancestry, as far as that can be judged by language—but not always.

---

2 The sons of Japheth; [285] Gomer,[286] and Magog,[287] and Madai,[288] and Javan,[289] and Tubal,[290] and Meshech,[291] and Tiras.[292]

---

285. These verses are part of the P-document and, as in the Creation-tale, the P-document organizes its material in such a way as to approach a climax. Thus, it starts

with Japheth, the youngest son of Noah, then moves on to Ham, and finally to Shem, who is the ancestor of the Israelites.

The names of the peoples and their locations would seem to represent the world as it existed in Assyrian times, in the seventh century B.C., or about a century before the Babylonian captivity.

Japheth himself may be borrowed from the Greek traditions, which reached the early Israelites by way of Crete and Cyprus and the Philistines. Japheth has been identified by some with Iapetus, one of the Titans in the Greek myths. The two names are almost identical, actually. If we discount the conventional "-us" ending in Greek names, both are pronounced "Yapet" in the original.

According to the Greek myths, Iapetus was the father of Prometheus, who, in turn, fathered the human race by molding them out of clay, as Yahveh did in the J-document. For this reason, Iapetus could be considered by the Greeks to be the ancestor of mankind; and the Israelites may have accepted this to the extent of making him the ancestor of that portion of mankind to which the Greeks belonged.

286. Gomer probably refers to the people who, in Assyrian inscriptions, are Gimirrai, and these, in turn, were the people known in Latin spelling as the Cimmerians. In earlier times, they lived north of the Black Sea (Crimea, part of their early homeland, is a distorted spelling of Cimmeria), but in the seventh century B.C., pushed on by new bands of tribesmen in the rear, they invaded Asia Minor and met the Assyrians there in great battles. The Cimmerians were eventually defeated, to be sure, but Assyria was badly wounded in the process. The Cimmerians were in particularly prominent view at the time this "table of nations" reached its final written form, and their eponymous ancestor, Gomer, would be viewed, very reasonably, as the firstborn of Japheth.

287. Magog may represent "the land of Gog." Gog ("Gyges" in the Greek form) was the king of the Lydians,

a people in western Asia Minor, and he was one of the important adversaries of the invading Cimmerians. In fact, he died in battle against them about 652 B.C.

288. Madai is supposed to refer to the Medes, who inhabited the territory east of Assyria and who were eventually among the final conquerors of Assyria.

289. Javan is a name that is very like an archaic form of the Greek Ion, who was the eponymous ancestor of the Ionian Greeks. The Ionians had migrated eastward, about 1000 B.C., to occupy the islands of the Aegean Sea and sections of the western coast of Asia Minor. Of the various Greek tribes, they were the nearest to the Israelites and would be best known to them in Assyrian times. Their tribal name would be naturally applied to the Greeks generally.

Thus, our word "Greek" is derived from the Latin. The Romans took the name of an obscure tribe they encountered in the west and applied it to all the Greeks generally. The Greeks called themselves Hellenes and considered themselves descended from an eponymous ancestor named Hellen, one of whose sons was Ion.

290. Tubal may be a reference to a tribe called Tibarenoi by Herodotus; this tribe dwelt in a region southeast of the Black Sea. Tubal-cain was a smith of that region, as I said earlier.

291. Meshech may be identified with a people called Mushki in Assyrian inscriptions. They had a king named Mita (Midas, in Greek), who ruled from 721 to 705 B.C. The reference could therefore be to the Phrygians, over whom Midas ruled and who dominated western Asia Minor until they were destroyed by the Cimmerians and replaced by the Lydians.

292. Tiras may be related to a people called by the Greeks Tyrsenoi. They were supposed to have fled Asia Minor and migrated to Italy. If so, Tiras could represent the Etruscans.

3 *And the sons of Gomer: Ashkenaz,* [293] *and Riphath, and Togarmah.*[294]

293. Ashkenaz may be identical with the name Ashguza, which is found among Assyrian inscriptions. This seems to refer to the people known to the Greeks as the Scythians, nomadic tribes who entered the regions north of the Black Sea from somewhere in central Asia some time before 1000 B.C. It was their pressure southward against the Cimmerians that drove the latter into Asia Minor. The Scythians took the Cimmerian place in the steppelands north of the Black Sea, and from that standpoint, Ashkenaz (Scythia) might well be considered the eldest son of Gomer (Cimmeria).

For some reason, the later Jews viewed Ashkenaz as the ancestor of the Teutonic people. Hence, Jews who spoke Yiddish (a form of German) were called *Ashkenazim* to distinguish them from those Jews who spoke Ladino (a form of Spanish) and who were called *Sephardim,* from *Sepharad,* a word taken by the Jews to refer to Spain.

294. Concerning Riphath, nothing at all is known or can be guessed. Some people equate Togarmah with a tribe known as Tilgarimmu to the Assyrians, a tribe that lived along the upper Euphrates.

4 *And the sons of Javan; Elishah,*[295] *and Tarshish,*[296] *Kittim,*[297] *and Dodanim.*[298]

295. Elishah is similar to the Alashiyah found in Assyrian documents, which refers to the island of Cyprus. This had already been colonized by Greeks in Assyrian times, and it was then the closest of all Greek-speaking lands to Canaan, being only two hundred miles to the northeast. The name, both in Hebrew and Assyrian, may

be a form of Hellas, the name the Greeks applied to the lands they populated.

296. Tarshish, in this verse, is most likely to represent Tarsus, an important Greek town on the southern coast of Asia Minor, a hundred miles north of Cyprus. It was already an important city in Assyrian times.

297. Kittim would seem to represent Kition, a city on the southern coast of Cyprus. Cyprus may thus be referred to twice in this verse.

298. Dodanim is widely thought to be a misprint for Rodanim, and in that case it might refer to the island of Rhodes, two hundred miles west of Cyprus. On the other hand, both Dodanim and Rodanim may be alternate spellings for a word that originally referred to Dardania, the region of northwestern Asia Minor where the city of Troy had stood prior to 1200 B.C.

---

5 *By these were the isles of the Gentiles[299] divided in their lands; every one after his tongue,[300] after their families, in their nations.*

---

299. "Gentiles" means "tribal people," from the Latin word *gens*, meaning "tribe." To the Israelites it came to mean, in particular, people who belonged to tribes other than their own, so that in the end, there came to be the distinction between Jew and Gentile. In a sense, though, the term Gentile can now be used by any group to refer to outsiders. Thus, Mormons today refer to non-Mormons (even Jews) as Gentiles.

"By these were the isles of the Gentiles divided in their lands" might be translated into present-day English thus: "The descendants of these migrated into and populated the various coastal lands."

Such a reading might indicate that they populated all

the coasts of the world including the Americas and Australia, but this is scarcely likely. The actual regions named in the guise of eponymous ancestors refer entirely to Asia Minor, to the islands off its coast, and, possibly, to the northern coast of the Black Sea. The Israelites of the time knew nothing beyond that.

300. It is assumed here that the descendants of Japheth spoke in different languages. This is difficult to understand, considering that all people were described as having been descended from a single family, that of Noah, in the not-too-distant past. The Biblical explanation of this is given in the next chapter.

---

6 *And the sons of Ham;* [301] *Cush,* [302] *and Mizraim,* [303] *and Phut,* [304] *and Canaan.* [305]

---

301. The P-document has gone as far as was thought necessary with the line of Japheth. It is dropped at this point, not to be resumed, and the P-document then passes on to the descendants of Ham.

302. In connection with Genesis 2:13, I explained the possible confusion between two lands to which Cush might refer: to Nubia, just south of Egypt, or to Kossea, just east of the Tigris River. Here the word undoubtedly refers to Nubia.

303. Mizraim is the Hebrew word for Egypt. Where it occurs in the Bible outside this chapter, Mizraim is translated into "Egypt," a term of Greek origin.

It may seem strange that Nubia is considered the oldest son of Ham, while Egypt, that ancient land of power and civilization, is placed second. However, at the time the "Table of Nations" was prepared, Egypt was in disarray and was under the rule of Nubia from 715 to 656 B.C.

304. Phut (better "Put," as given in the Revised Standard Version) is usually thought to represent the peoples west of Egypt, whom the Greeks called Libyans.

305. Canaan is, of course, the land later dominated by Israel. If we translate Genesis 10:6 into modern geographic language, it would read: "And the sons of Ham: Nubia, Egypt, Libya, and Canaan." This actually marks the extent of the Egyptian Empire in the times of its greatness between 1800 and 1200 B.C.

The languages of Nubia, Egypt, and Libya were, in Biblical times, similar and belonged to the same linguistic family (Hamitic). The language of the Canaanites, however, was quite different and was, indeed, related to Hebrew. The Canaanites, therefore, spoke what we would now call a Semitic language, and if language were indeed the criterion for determining descent, Canaan would have to be accounted a descendant of Shem.

Yet the compilers of the Table of Nations considered political connection rather than language the criterion and, besides, had an interest in not making the Canaanite-Israelite relationship too close or there would be trouble in justifying the Canaanite conquest and enslavement.

---

7 And the sons of Cush; 306 Seba, and Havilah, and Sabtah, and Raamah, and Sabtecha: and the sons of Raamah; Sheba, and Dedan.

---

306. The five sons and two grandsons of Cush here represent regions that are almost certainly located in various parts of Arabia. There were occasions in ancient times when regions on the Arabian shore of the Red Sea dominated the African shore, and vice versa. This verse could conceivably reflect the memory of this connection between Nubia and Arabia.

8 *And Cush begat Nimrod:*[307] *he began to be*
a mighty one in the earth.[308]

307. At this point, the J-document takes over. The Biblical editors apparently interrupted the dry P-document listing of names whenever something colorful could be found in the J-document.

308. Nimrod was, apparently, a ruler and conqueror.

9 *He was a mighty hunter before the*
Lord: [309] *wherefore it is said, Even as Nim-*
rod the mighty hunter before the Lord.

309. To be "a mighty hunter before the Lord" is an idiomatic way of saying "to be a very great hunter." Apparently, Nimrod's feats became proverbial.

As we are to see in the next verse, the scene of his exploits was the Tigris-Euphrates valley, and hunting was a favorite pursuit of the Assyrian monarchs. Assyrian art was powerful, and one of the favorite objects of portrayal was that of Assyrian kings in pursuit of big game.

One of the first of the great Assyrian conquerors was Tukulti-Ninurta I, who reigned from 1244 to 1208 B.C. From his home base in Assyria on the upper Tigris, he extended his sway northward into Urartu and southward into Babylonia.

The Greeks to the west may have heard vague tales of his conquests (just prior to the Trojan War), for in later times they told of a conquering king whom they called Ninus, a Greek form of the second part of Tukulti-Ninurta's name, and who, they said, founded the Assyrian Empire. It may be that the Israelites also knew of these early conquests and that to them Tukulti-Ninurta became Nimrod.

10 *And the beginning of his kingdom was Babel,[310] and Erech,[311] and Accad,[312] and Calneh,[313] in the land of Shinar.[314]*

310. The important towns of Nimrod's realm are listed. Babel is better known by the Greek version of its name, Babylon. Babylon was a small and unremarkable village until about 1900 B.C., when a tribe from the middle Euphrates, the Amorites, seized control and made it the capital of an expanding empire.

Under the sixth king of the Amorite dynasty, Hammurabi, who reigned about 1700 B.C., Babylon became a world metropolis and remained one for two thousand years.

311. Erech is the city of Uruk, located on the lower Euphrates. It dates back to 3600 B.C. at least, and was one of the important Sumerian city-states. The mythical Gilgamesh was once king of this city, and it was ruled by a historical conqueror, Lugal-zaggisi, shortly after 2300 B.C. Lugal-zaggisi was the first person we know of to rule a sizable empire in the Tigris-Euphrates region.

312. Accad, or Akkad, is, in the ancient inscriptions, Agade. Its exact site is unknown, but it was probably on the Euphrates about 140 miles upstream from Uruk.

The Akkadians were at first under Sumerian domination, but about 2280 B.C., an Akkadian ruler, Sargon of Agade, came to power. He expanded his dominions, and in 2264 B.C., he defeated Lugal-zaggisi to found an Akkadian Empire.

313. The location of Calneh is unknown, and there is general agreement now that its inclusion is an error and that the word is not the name of a city but is Hebrew for "all of them." The verse is made to read in the Revised Standard Version: "The beginning of his kingdom was

Babel, Erech, and Accad, all of them in the land of Shinar."

314. There is general agreement that "the land of Shinar" is Sumeria and, more generally, the Tigris-Euphrates region.

---

11 *Out of that land went forth Asshur,*[315] *and builded Nineveh,*[316] *and the city Rehoboth,*[317] *and Calah,*[318]

---

315. The beginning of this verse is now generally accepted as distortion due to the accidental omission of a pronoun in the Hebrew. The Revised Standard Version has the verse begin: "Out of that land he went forth into Asshur," where the "he" refers to Nimrod.

Asshur is the region along the upper courses of the Tigris River. The town of Asshur, which gave its name to the region, was located on the Tigris about 230 miles north of Babylon; it was founded as early as 2700 B.C. Asshur is far better known by the Greek version of its name, Assyria.

Assyria was part of the Akkadian Empire and then, later, part of the Amorite Empire. When the Amorites fell before the invading Kassites (the Middle Eastern Cush), Assyria became an independent region with its capital at Asshur.

316. Nineveh was the capital of Assyria in the last century of its existence. Although it did not exist (or was, at best, a small village) before 700 B.C., it was during the following century that Assyria was at its mightiest and was overlord of Judea. To the later Jews, Nineveh was the very epitome of Assyria and is bound to be mentioned at once.

317. Rehoboth is unknown as a city, except for the mention in this verse. The word may be a distortion of a

phrase meaning "broad streets." The phrase "Nineveh, and the city Rehoboth" might, perhaps, more accurately be translated as "Nineveh, a city of broad streets."

318. Asshur was the first capital of Assyria when it was an obscure nation. The Assyrian king Shalmaneser I (the father of Tukulti-Ninurta I) built a new capital at Calah, about twenty miles south of the eventual site of Nineveh. The verse thus mentions the three capitals of Assyria: Asshur, Calah, and Nineveh.

---

12 *And Resen[319] between Nineveh and Calah: the same is a great city.[320]*

---

319. No city by the name of Resen or anything like it can be found in the ancient inscriptions. A word something like "Resen" refers to some sort of water reservoir, and it may be, conceivably, that the Bible is referring to such a reservoir or an aqueduct between the two chief cities of the later Assyrian Empire.

320. The "great city" is not a reference to Resen, but to either Nineveh or Calah or, possibly, both.

The whole passage in verses 8 through 12 is a very brief and very garbled résumé of the history of the Tigris-Euphrates region stretching over a period of about twenty-five hundred years. It covers Sumeria (Erech), Akkad (Accad), the Amorites (Babel), and Assyria (Asshur, Calah, and Nineveh). Nimrod, in whose name all this is recited, seems to be a telescoped memory of a number of the conquerors of the region: Gilgamesh, Lugal-zaggisi, Sargon, Shalmaneser, Tukulti-Ninurta.

---

13 *And Mizraim begat Ludim, and Anamim, and Lehabim, and Naphtuhim.[321]*

---

321. Presumably these names are all associated with regions in or near Egypt (Mizraim), but what or who they are cannot be determined.

---

14 *And Pathrusim, and Casluhim,*[322] *(out of whom came Philistim*[323]*) and Caphtorim.*[324]

---

322. Pathrusim and Casluhim, like the Ludim, Anamim, Lehabim, and Naphtuhim of the previous verse, have the -im suffix of the Hebrew plural. They are not the names of people or of eponymous ancestors, but the names of tribes. All these tribes are Egyptian-related.

323. The Casluhim are here reported to be the ancestors of the Philistim, a Hebrew word elsewhere translated as "Philistines."

The Philistines controlled the southern coast of Canaan in later times and were important enemies of Israel during the time of the Judges and of King Saul. They are here listed among the descendants of Ham and are particularly related to Egypt.

Actually, in the thirteenth century B.C., toward the closing days of the decaying Egyptian Empire, there were barbarian invasions descending on the Egyptian coastline. The Egyptians called them "the Peoples of the Sea" and beat them off, in the process just about consuming the last energies of the Empire. The Peoples of the Sea, ricocheting off Egypt, so to speak, settled on the Canaanite Coast (as the Philistines) just as the Israelites were entering Canaan from the east. The Israelites, noting that they came from Egypt, considered them descended from Mizraim.

It is generally felt that the Philistines were, at least in part, of Greek descent, so that it might have been more appropriate to make them descendants of Japheth rather than Ham. (Similarly, since Nimrod was related to the Middle Eastern Cush, at least geographically, rather than the Nubian Cush, he should have been made a descendant of Shem, rather than of Ham.)

324. Although this verse states the Philistines to have descended from Mizraim by way of the Casluhim, there are later references in the Bible that make it seem they descended by way of the Caphtorim. The Philistines are spoken of as "the remnant of the country of Caphtor" (Jeremiah 47:4), and there is also mention of "the Philistines from Caphtor" (Amos 9:7).

The trouble is that we don't know where Caphtor is. There have been suggestions that it was Cyprus, Crete, the southern coast of Asia Minor. Perhaps all these regions contributed contingents to the Peoples of the Sea, but which particular one the Biblical writers had in mind we cannot say. (Most of the confusion in this chapter arises from the J-document, more flamboyant and legendary, rather than from the sober P-document.)

---

15 *And Canaan begat Sidon his firstborn,*[325] *and Heth,*[326]

---

325. Canaan is pictured as the father of the various Canaanite tribes. Since these are known in detail to the Israelites, numerous descendants are listed.

Sidon is a city on the Mediterranean, about 130 miles north of Jerusalem. The area about it is now known as Lebanon and was known to the Greeks as Phoenicia.

Since the Phoenicians were never conquered by the Israelites, and since Sidon was the strongest of the Phoenician towns during the Israelite Monarchic period, Sidon is listed as the firstborn of Canaan.

326. Heth is the eponymous ancestor of the Hittites, who are sometimes referred to in the Bible as the "sons of Heth." Because the Hittites are invariably mentioned in the Bible as among the tribes of Canaanite, one might feel they were a minor people.

The old Egyptian and Babylonian records, however, speak of the Kheta or Khatti (names quite similar to Heth, when all are pronounced in their native tongues) as a powerful people north of Canaan.

It turns out that there was a strong Hittite Empire that ruled over eastern Asia Minor and that was strong enough to fight the Egyptian Empire on equal terms and to do somewhat more than hold its own.

The Hittite Empire declined and decayed, however, and only small remnants of Hittite centers were left at the time the Israelites conquered Canaan. It seemed by then that they were indeed a minor tribe, and their earlier greatness went unnoticed in the Bible.

16 *And the Jebusite,[327] and the Amorite,[328] and the Girgasite,[329]*

327. The further descendants of Canaan are not listed as individuals but as tribes. The Jebusites are a tribe whose prize possession was the town that King David, in later times, captured, fortified, and made his capital—Jerusalem.

328. The Amorites were a powerful tribe that ruled the Tigris-Euphrates region between 1700 and 1500 B.C. By the time the Israelites conquered Canaan, however, there were only relics of the Amorites left, as of the Hittites. Like the Hittites, the Amorites appear as a minor tribe with no reference to their past greatness.

329. Nothing is known of the Girgasites.

17 *And the Hivite,[330] and the Arkite,[331] and the Sinite,[332]*

330. The Hivites may well be the Hurrians, who established the kingdom of Mitanni in the upper Tigris-Eu-

phrates and who flourished between 1475 and 1275 B.C. They were then conquered by the Hittites, just before both were shattered and absorbed in the first wave of Assyrian conquest. Again, the Israelites found only remnants and reported them as a minor tribe.

331. Arkites were the people of Arka, a town in Phoenicia.

332. Sinites seem to have been people of Sianna, a place near Arka.

---

18 *And the Arvadite,[333] and the Zemarite,[334] and the Hamathite:[335] and afterward were the families of the Canaanites spread abroad.*

---

333. Arvadites were the inhabitants of the Phoenician city of Arvad.

334. Zemarites are the inhabitants of Simarra, another place near Arka.

335. Hamathites are the inhabitants of Hamath, a city in Syria.

---

19 *And the border of the Canaanites[336] was from Sidon, as thou comest to Gerar,[337] unto Gaza;[338] as thou goest, unto Sodom,[339] and Gomorrah, and Admah, and Zeboim, even unto Lasha.[340]*

---

336. The Biblical writers, having detailed the tribal content of Canaan minutely, are interested in establishing its exact extent ("the border of the Canaanites") since it became the Israelite homeland.

337. Gerar is in southern Canaan, about 150 miles south of Sidon and about eighteen miles inland from the coast.

338. Gaza is about as far south as Gerar but is located on the coast. In other words, Canaan is described here as having a north-south extension of 150 miles, not very much by modern standards, but quite ample in a day when people usually traveled by walking.

339. Having established the north-south extension, it is next necessary to establish the east-west extension.

Sodom, Gomorrah, Admah, and Zeboim were in the southeast of Canaan. Their exact site is not known, for they were destroyed in some disaster at some early time (an event described in the nineteenth chapter of Genesis). These cities were supposed to have existed in the region of the Dead Sea, however, and some even speculate that they might be covered by the southernmost extension of the Dead Sea, that area having been flooded after an earthquake or volcanic eruption, which inspired the Biblical tale of the destruction.

If we assume Sodom to be somewhere in the south of the Dead Sea, then the east-west extension from Gaza to Sodom is about 65 miles.

340. Lasha is mentioned only here in the Bible, and its location is unknown. It is just possible, however, that the town that is meant is Laish, later called Dan, about twenty-seven miles southeast of Sidon.

If that is so, then Canaan is described as a roughly rectangular patch of ground on the southeastern shore of the Mediterranean with an area of somewhat under ten thousand square miles. It would be something like the size and shape of an upside-down Vermont.

---

20 *These are the sons of Ham, after their families, after their tongues, in their countries, and in their nations.*

21 Unto Shem also,[341] the father of all the children of Eber,[342] the brother of Japheth the elder,[343] even to him were children born.

---

341. The genealogies of Japheth and Ham are done, and now the Table of Nations passes on to Shem.

342. Shem is identified as the ancestor of Eber, the eponymous ancestor of the Hebrews, among whom are the Israelites.

343. This phrase makes it look as if Japheth is the older brother of Shem, but in all other mentions of the sons of Noah, it is clear that Shem is the oldest. The King James here misphrases the matter. The Revised Standard Version has the verse read: "To Shem also, the father of all the children of Eber, the elder brother of Japheth, children were born."

---

22 The children of Shem; Elam,[344] and Asshur,[345] and Arphaxad,[346] and Lud,[347] and Aram.[348]

---

344. Elam was a nation at the northern end of the Persian Gulf, just east of the Tigris River. It entered history in Sumerian times and remained a strong rival of whatever nation dominated the Tigris-Euphrates valley right through Assyrian times.

345. Asshur is, of course, Assyria. Here its eponymous ancestor is made a descendant of Shem by the P-document. Linguistically, this is more correct than was its association with Nimrod, who was pictured as a descendant of Ham by the J-document, eleven verses earlier.

346. What the name Arphaxad represents is not clear. It is the only name in this verse that does not clearly

represent a nation, and it is the one of the five children of Shem who is in the direct line of ancestry of the Israelites. (From the time of Seth onward, this is the first time in which the Israelites describe one of their ancestors as anything but the eldest son of his father. Arphaxad is the third son.)

347. Lud is usually interpreted as representing Lydia, but Lydia has already been noted as being represented by Magog, twenty verses back, and it makes more sense to suppose Lydia to have been of Japhetic descent than of Semitic. But then what does Lud represent? It's a problem.

348. Aram is the eponymous ancestor of the Aramaeans, a tribe that emerged from northern Arabia about 1100 B.C. and whose raids weakened Assyria for a period after the conquering times of Tukulti-Ninurta I. Eventually, an Aramaean kingdom maintained itself north of Canaan; it is better known by the Greek name of Syria.

---

23 *And the children of Aram; Uz, and Hul, and Gether, and Mash.*[349]

---

349. The four sons of Aram represent, presumably, four Aramaean subtribes, districts, or cities, but which they may be, no one has been able to work out convincingly.

---

24 *And Arphaxad begat Salah; and Salah begat Eber.*[350]

---

350. This represents the line of descent of the Israelites.

25 *And unto Eber were born two sons: the name of one was Peleg; for in his days was the earth divided;*[351] *and his brother's name was Joktan.*[352]

351. The name Peleg is similar to the Hebrew word *palag,* meaning "to divide," and this explanation of the name may be a bit of folk-etymology with no clear significance. It may, however, be a reference to the legend recounted in the next chapter.

352. It is Peleg, and not Joktan, who is in the direct line of ancestry of the Israelites. Therefore, the descendants of Joktan are given and done with in the following verses.

26 *And Joktan begat Almodad, and Sheleph, and Hazarmaveth, and Jerah,*

27 *And Hadoram, and Uzal, and Diklah,*

28 *And Obal, and Abimael, and Sheba,*

29 *And Ophir, and Havilah, and Jobab:* [353] *all these were the sons of Joktan.*

353. Thirteen sons of Joktan are listed, representing, presumably, thirteen related tribes or, at any rate, thirteen closely grouped tribes of similar language and culture. It is thought that the sons of Joktan represent tribes dwelling in southern Arabia.

30 *And their dwelling was from Mesha, as thou goest unto Sephar a mount of the east.*[354]

354. Neither Mesha nor Sephar are mentioned elsewhere in the Bible, and neither locality can be pinpointed.

31 *These are the sons of Shem, after their families, after their tongues, in their lands, after their nations.*

32 *These are the families of the sons of Noah, after their generations, in their nations: and by these were the nations divided in the earth after the flood.*

Chapter 11

1 *And the whole earth was of one language, and of one speech.*[355]

355. If, indeed, all of mankind existed as a single family immediately after the Flood, then, indeed, they and, for that matter, their immediate descendants would all speak a single language.

In actual fact, in the twenty-fourth century B.C., the traditional time of the Flood, there was undoubtedly a multiplicity of languages already existing on the Earth even over the restricted area known to the Middle-Eastern civilizations of the time. Sumerian, Akkadian, and Egyptian were fundamentally different from each other, and there were undoubtedly hundreds, if not thousands, of other languages in existence outside the Middle East, all mutually unintelligible.

We have no knowledge of when human speech drifted apart into separate languages. For one thing, we don't know when the ability of speech originated and by what steps a formal language was developed. It is quite likely we will never know, but it seems reasonable to suppose that languages were already differentiated thousands of years before civilization began.

2 *And it came to pass, as they journeyed from the east,*[356] *that they found a plain in the land of Shinar;*[357] *and they dwelt there.*

356. The phrase "from the east" would make it seem as though the Sumerians entered the Tigris-Euphrates valley from the east; indeed, they may have done so. At least, they may have earlier inhabited the mountainous regions along the northeastern banks of the Tigris.

However, if the ark had come to rest in Ararat anywhere near the traditional spot, then the descendants of Noah, in entering Sumeria, would have drifted in from the northwest.

The Bible, however, doesn't actually speak definitely in this matter. The phrase "from the east" in the King James Version may not be quite accurate. The Revised Standard Version has the verse read: "And as men migrated in the east . . ."

"East" to the Biblical writers always meant "east of Canaan," so the reference is to a migration out there in the eastern lands (of which Sumeria was part) without reference to where the migration was coming from.

357. In the previous chapter, it is said of Nimrod: ". . . the beginning of his kingdom was . . . in the land of Shinar." It is often assumed for this reason that the event about to be described takes place during the reign of Nimrod and that he was the driving force behind it. However, the Bible doesn't specifically say so.

3 *And they said one to another, Go to, let us make brick, and burn them thoroughly.*[358] *And they had brick for stone, and slime* [359] *had they for mortar.*

358. In prehistoric times, moist clay was used to daub

woven baskets. Dried in the sun, the clay made it possible for the baskets to carry liquids. Such daubed baskets, if left too close to a campfire, may have hardened further, and more or less accidentally, it was discovered that if clay was baked, it became a sort of artificial stone. In this way, bricks and pottery came into use.

The oldest such fire-baked clay has indeed been found in the region that eventually became Sumeria and dates back to about 6500 B.C., some four thousand years before the traditional date of the Flood.

359. The Hebrew word translated as "slime" here is more properly translated "bitumen" (as it is in the Revised Standard Version) or as "pitch." Bitumen is a soft, sticky, waterproof black solid; hydrocarbon in nature. Chemically, it is related to petroleum; petroleum from which the more easily evaporated fractions are gone.

The Middle East, as we all know today, is rich in underground oil. Some of it seeps to the surface and partially evaporates, leaving the bitumen behind. Bitumen serves not only as a waterproofing agent, but as a mortar, too, making bricks stick together and forming a wall that is all one piece.

---

4 *And they said, Go to, let us build us a city and a tower,[360] whose top may reach unto heaven; [361] and let us make a name, lest we be scattered abroad [362] upon the face of the whole earth.*

---

360. Agricultural peoples did tend to build cities for self-protection, and these would include towers. A tower could serve as a lookout point from which the approach of an enemy could be seen and an early warning be given. If strongly built, it could serve as a citadel, a refuge for noncombatants, the place for a last stand.

361. A tower could also be a place of worship. Since it was common to worship sun-gods, sky-gods, and storm-gods, one would try to get closer to the homes of these

gods in the sky, in order that the prayers, and the scent of the sacrifices, would have a better chance of reaching their target.

In hilly regions, it would be reasonable to set up an altar on a hilltop. Perhaps the Sumerians did so in the hilly land in which they lived before they migrated to the Tigris-Euphrates. In the flat plain of that region, they may well have felt it necessary to build an artificial hill if they were to expect their religious rites to be noticed by the gods. It is for that reason they might build a tower, and in that sense they would hope that its "top may reach unto heaven."

362. If a tower were not built, it might follow that through inability to mount a strong defense (in the case of a military tower) or to mobilize divine forces (in the case of a religious tower), the people would not make "a name" for themselves; that is, become famous as successful warriors. In that case, they might be driven from the land and "scattered abroad."

---

5 *And the Lord came down to see the city and the tower,*[363] *which the children of men builded.*

---

363. We have here another primitive tale of the J-document in which God is pictured as though he had limited powers. He must come down to Earth to see the city and tower.

---

6 *And the Lord said, Behold, the people is one, and they have all one language; and this they begin to do; and now nothing will be restrained from them, which they have imagined to do.*[364]

---

364. God seems to be described here as fearing the powers of united humanity. One gets the impression that

God is angered by human presumption in daring to try to build something high enough to reach heaven (if the phrase is accepted literally, rather than metaphorically). If so, the tone of this verse is rather that of God fearing that humanity will attempt to storm heaven and conquer it and that he, God, must take measures quickly to prevent it.

It is, of course, possible to interpret it otherwise—that God does not wish human beings to undertake foolish tasks beyond their capacity (and there would be many who would apply the lesson to the present time). But that requires interpretation. The literal words present a primitive picture of the Deity.

---

7 *Go to, let us* [365] *go down, and there confound their language, that they may not understand one another's speech.* [366]

---

365. This would seem to be another remnant of an ancient polytheistic outlook that the Biblical editors could not, or did not, remove.

366. By proceeding to "confound their language" (that is, have different people speak different languages), God destroys the unity of humanity, performing a kind of mental descent into Chaos equivalent to the physical descent of the Flood.

---

8 *So the Lord scattered them abroad from thence upon the face of all the earth: and they left off to build the city.* [367]

---

367. In particular, one presumes, they were unable to continue building the tower.

The Sumerians did build towers for religious purposes, and these were called ziggurats (their word for "pinnacle" or "mountain peak"). One of them was ordered begun by a Sumerian king and was left unfinished, perhaps as a result of the disorders involved in the wars of Sargon of Agade. For centuries, this ziggurat remained incomplete and perhaps gained fame because of its shortcoming (as does the Leaning Tower of Pisa or Schubert's Unfinished Symphony). It may be that this unfinished ziggurat served as the model for the tale of the unfinished tower.

---

9 *Therefore is the name of it called Babel; because the Lord did there confound the language of all the earth:* [368] *and from thence did the Lord scatter them abroad upon the face of all the earth.*

---

368. The Biblical theory is that Babel was called that from the Hebrew word *balal,* meaning "to mix" or "to confuse." This is a bit of folk-etymology that is flat wrong. "Babel" is the Hebrew version of the Babylonian *Bab-ilu,* meaning "the gate of God."

There was an unfinished ziggurat in Babel (Babylon) at that, though it may not have been the one that originally inspired the legend, which is probably quite an old one. It was, however, the one in Babylon that caused the writers of the P-document to place the legendary tower there, perhaps.

The unfinished ziggurat in Babylon was called *Etemenanki,* meaning "house of the foundation of heaven and earth." In the sixth century B.C., Nebuchadnezzar, who ruled Babylon at its peak of greatness, finished it (or perhaps rebuilt it). It was the largest ziggurat ever built. It was formed in seven diminishing stages (one for each of the planets). The bottommost stage was about 300 feet square, and the whole thing reared 325 feet into the air. Building it was a remarkable feat, considering the state of the art at the time; it was the largest structure of its day in southwestern Asia.

Although there are many people who know of the unfinished "tower of Babel," there are probably few who know that it was eventually finished.

---

10 These are the generations of Shem: [369] Shem was an hundred years old,[370] and begat Arphaxad two years after the flood: [371]

---

369. We now return to the P-document, which takes up the genealogy of Shem, carrying it down to the founding of the Israelite line.

370. Noah was five hundred years old when his children were born, and Shem was his oldest son. Since the Flood came when Noah was six hundred years old, Shem was one hundred when the Flood began. The genealogy, in other words, begins with the Flood.

371. The Flood lasted a year, according to the P-document, so Shem was 103 years old when Arphaxad was born.

---

11 And Shem lived after he begat Arphaxad five hundred years,[372] and begat sons and daughters.

---

372. Shem died, in other words, at the age of 603. His lifetime was not quite two-thirds that of his father, Noah, and the ages now continue to grow steadily shorter.

---

12 And Arphaxad lived five and thirty years, and begat Salah:

13 And Arphaxad lived after he begat Salah four hundred and three years, and begat sons and daughters.

14 *And Salah lived thirty years, and begat Eber:*

15 *And Salah lived after he begat Eber four hundred and three years, and begat sons and daughters.*

16 *And Eber lived four and thirty years, and begat Peleg:* [373]

---

373. If we add up the ages of these "postdiluvian patriarchs" at the time they had their children, it will turn out that Peleg was born 102 years after the beginning of the Flood, or 1,758 years after the Creation; that is, in 2246 B.C. At that time, Noah was still alive, for he lived 350 years after the Flood.

---

17 *And Eber lived after he begat Peleg four hundred and thirty years, and begat sons and daughters.*

18 *And Peleg lived thirty years, and begat Reu:*

19 *And Peleg lived after he begat Reu two hundred and nine years,[374] and begat sons and daughters.*

---

374. Peleg died at the age of 239; that is, in 2007 B.C. Noah was still alive at that time, being 940 years old. He outlived Peleg by ten years, dying in 1998 B.C.

If the statement in Genesis 10:25, that in Peleg's time the earth was divided, refers to the Tower of Babel, then that would imply that the tower was in the process of being built sometime between 2247 and 2008 B.C. This period is in late Sumerian times, and that is a reasonable statement—for the building of the tower, though not for the confounding of the language.

20 *And Reu lived two and thirty years and begat Serug:*

21 *And Reu lived after he begat Serug two hundred and seven years, and begat sons and daughters.*

22 *And Serug lived thirty years, and begat Nahor:*

23 *And Serug lived after he begat Nahor two hundred years, and begat sons and daughters.*

24 *And Nahor lived nine and twenty years, and begat Terah:*

25 *And Nahor lived after he begat Terah an hundred and nineteen years, and begat sons and daughters.*

26 *And Terah lived seventy years, and begat Abram,[375] Nahor,[376] and Haran.[377]*

---

375. Abram, later called Abraham, is the direct ancestor of the Israelites and some related tribes.

By adding up the years in this chapter, it would seem that Abram was born in 2055 B.C., at which time Noah was still alive. In fact, Noah doesn't die until Abram is fifty-seven years old. Shem is also still alive. Since Shem lived 502 years after the Flood, he outlived Abram by thirty-five years, dying in 1845 B.C. (Noah and Shem must have been painfully puzzled by the decreasing life-span of their descendants.)

376. Nahor is mentioned because his daughter will marry Abraham's son, and his granddaughter will marry Abraham's grandson, so that he, too, is a direct ancestor of the Israelites. Nahor is exceptional in one respect. Most of the names in the Bible are unique, and there are few cases of two individuals bearing the same name. Nahor is an exception since he bears the name of his grandfather.

377. Haran is named since his son will be involved with Abram in later chapters.

---

27 *Now these are the generations of Terah: Terah begat Abram, Nahor, and Haran; and Haran begat Lot.*[378]

---

378. Lot, Abram's nephew, is the one who will be involved with him in later chapters and who will be described as the ancestor of the Moabites and Ammonites, neighbors and enemies of the Israelites.

---

28 *And Haran died before his father Terah in the land of his nativity, in Ur*[379] *of the Chaldees.*[380]

---

379. The J-document takes up the tale now.

Ur was a Sumerian city, founded no later than 3500 B.C. and located on the right bank of the Euphrates River about 140 miles southeast of Babylon, right at what was then the coastline of the Persian Gulf.

It was eclipsed by Lugal-zaggisi and Sargon of Agade, but after their empires were gone, Ur entered another period of commercial prosperity under its "third dynasty" between 2050 and 1950 B.C., and Abram was born just about at the beginning of this period.

380. By the time the Bible reached its written form, Ur was a decayed and obscure village. It had to be defined as "Ur of the Chaldees" (or Chaldeans); that is "Ur, a city in the Chaldean territory." The Chaldeans were an Arabian tribe who became dominant in what had once been Sumeria in 1150 B.C. Abram's Ur flourished seven centuries before the Chaldeans arrived, but to the readers of the Bible when it was first reduced to writing, the land was Chaldean territory.

29 *And Abram and Nahor took them wives: the name of Abram's wife was Sarai; and the name of Nahor's wife, Milcah, the daughter of Haran, the father of Milcah, and the father of Iscah.*

30 *But Sarai was barren; she had no child.*

31 *And Terah took Abram his son, and Lot the son of Haran his son's son, and Sarai his daughter in law, his son Abram's wife; and they went forth with them from Ur of the Chaldees, to go into the land of Canaan; and they came unto Haran,[381] and dwelt there.*

381. The normal trade routes from Ur to Canaan followed a curve of fertile land, going first northwest and then southwest (the "fertile crescent") thus skirting the Arabian desert. Haran, or Charan, was an important city on the northern peak of the fertile crescent. To the Greeks and Romans it was known as Carrhae. It is located on the eastern bank of the Balikh River, which flows south into the upper Euphrates, sixty miles away. It is in what is now southeastern Turkey, just north of the Syrian border.

32 *And the days of Terah were two hundred and five years:[382] and Terah died in Haran.*

382. Terah is the last person in the Bible who is specifically said to have lived more than two hundred years. If we follow the figures of the P-document, he died in 1921 B.C., when Abram was 135 years old. Shem and Arphaxad were still alive at the death of Terah.

With this, the Biblical account of primeval history comes to an end.

Appendix

Primeval History According to the P-Document

In the beginning God created the heaven and the earth. And the earth was without form, and void; and darkness was upon the face of the deep. And the Spirit of God moved upon the face of the waters. And God´said, Let there be light: and there was light. And God saw the light, that it was good: and God divided the light from the darkness. And God called the light Day, and the darkness he called Night. And the evening and the morning were the first day.

And God said, Let there be a firmament in the midst of the waters, and let it divide the waters from the waters. And God made the firmament, and divided the waters which were under the firmament from the waters which were above the firmament: and it was so. And God called the firmament Heaven. And the evening and the morning were the second day.

And God said, Let the waters under the heaven be gathered together unto one place, and let the dry land appear: and it was so. And God called the dry land Earth; and the gathering together of the waters called he Seas: and God saw that it was good. And God said, Let the earth bring forth grass, the herb yielding seed, and the fruit tree yielding fruit after his kind, whose seed is in itself, upon the earth: and it was so. And the earth brought forth grass, and herb yielding seed after his kind, and the tree yielding fruit, whose seed was in itself, after his kind: and God saw that it was good. And the evening and the morning were the third day.

And God said, Let there be lights in the firmament of the heaven to divide the day from the night; and let them be for signs, and for seasons, and for days, and years: And let them be for lights in the firmament of the heaven to give light upon the earth: and it was so. And God made two great lights; the greater light to rule the day, and the lesser light to rule the night: he made the stars also. And God set them in the firmament of the heaven to give light upon the earth, and to rule over the day and over the night, and to divide the light from the darkness: and God saw that it was good. And the evening and the morning were the fourth day.

And God said, Let the waters bring forth abundantly the moving creature that hath life, and fowl that may fly above the earth in the open firmament of heaven. And God created great whales, and every living creature that moveth, which the waters brought forth abundantly, after their kind, and every winged fowl after his kind: and God saw that it was good. And God blessed them, saying, Be fruitful, and multiply, and fill the waters in the seas, and let fowl multiply in the earth. And the evening and the morning were the fifth day.

And God said, Let the earth bring forth the living creature after his kind, cattle, and creeping thing, and beast of the earth after his kind: and it was so. And God made the beast of the earth after his kind, and cattle after their kind, and every thing that creepeth upon the earth after his kind: and God saw that it was good.

And God said, Let us make man in our image, after our likeness: and let them have dominion over the fish of the sea, and over the fowl of the air, and over the cattle, and over all the earth, and over every creeping thing that creepeth upon the earth. So God created man in his own image, in the image of God created he him; male and female created he them. And God blessed them, and God said unto them, Be fruitful, and multiply, and replenish the earth, and subdue it: and have dominion over the fish of the sea, and over the fowl of the air, and over every living thing that moveth upon the earth.

And God said, Behold, I have given you every herb bearing seed, which is upon the face of all the earth, and every tree, in the which is the fruit of a tree yielding seed; to you it shall be for meat. And to every beast of the earth, and to every fowl of the air, and to every thing that creepeth upon the earth, wherein there is life, I have given every green herb for meat: and it was so. And God saw every thing that he had made, and, behold, it was very good. And the evening and the morning were the sixth day.

Thus the heavens and the earth were finished, and all the host of them. And on the seventh day God ended his work which he had made; and he rested on the seventh day from all his work which he had made. And God blessed the seventh day, and sanctified it: because that in it he had rested from all his work which God created and made.

These are the generations of the heavens and of the earth when they were created.

This is the book of the generations of Adam. In the day that God created man, in the likeness of God made he him; male and female created he them; and blessed them, and called their name Adam, in the day when they were created.

And Adam lived an hundred and thirty years, and begat a son in his own likeness, after his image; and called his name Seth: And the days of Adam after he had begotten Seth were eight hundred years: and he begat sons and daughters: and all the days that Adam lived were nine hundred and thirty years: and he died.

And Seth lived an hundred and five years, and begat Enos: and Seth lived after he begat Enos eight hundred and seven years, and begat sons and daughters: and all the days of Seth were nine hundred and twelve years: and he died.

And Enos lived ninety years, and begat Cainan: and Enos lived after he begat Cainan eight hundred and fifteen years, and begat sons and daughters: and all the days of Enos were nine hundred and five years: and he died.

And Cainan lived seventy years, and begat Mahalaleel: and Cainan lived after he begat Mahalaleel eight hundred and forty years, and begat sons and daughters: and all the days of Cainan were nine hundred and ten years: and he died.

And Mahalaleel lived sixty and five years, and begat Jared: and Mahalaleel lived after he begat Jared eight hundred and thirty years, and begat sons and daughters: and all the days of Mahalaleel were eight hundred ninety and five years: and he died.

And Jared lived an hundred sixty and two years, and he begat Enoch: and Jared lived after he begat Enoch eight hundred years, and begat sons and daughters: and all the days of Jared were nine hundred sixty and two years: and he died.

And Enoch lived sixty and five years and begat Methuselah: and Enoch walked with God after he begat Methuselah three hundred years, and begat sons and daughters: and all the days of Enoch were three hundred sixty and five years: and Enoch walked with God: and he was not; for God took him.

And Methuselah lived an hundred eighty and seven years, and begat Lamech: and Methuselah lived after he begat Lamech seven hundred eighty and two years, and begat sons and daughters: and all the days of Methuselah were nine hundred sixty and nine years: and he died.

And Lamech lived an hundred eighty and two years, and begat a son [Noah]: and Lamech lived after he begat Noah five hundred ninety and five years, and begat sons and daughters: and all the days of Lamech were seven hundred seventy and seven years: and he died.

And Noah was five hundred years old: and Noah begat Shem, Ham, and Japheth.

These are the generations of Noah: Noah was a just man and perfect in his generations, and Noah walked with God. And Noah begat three sons, Shem, Ham and Japheth.

The earth also was corrupt before God, and the earth was filled with violence. And God looked upon the earth, and, behold, it was corrupt; for all flesh had corrupted his way upon the earth.

And God said unto Noah, The end of all flesh is come before me; for the earth is filled with violence through them; and, behold, I will destroy them with the earth.

Make thee an ark of gopher wood; rooms shalt thou make in the ark, and shalt pitch it within and without with pitch. And this is the fashion which thou shalt make it of: The length of the ark shall be three hundred cubits, the breadth of it fifty cubits, and the height of it thirty cubits. A window shalt thou make to the ark, and in a cubit shalt thou finish it above; and the door of the ark shalt thou set in the side thereof; with lower, second, and third stories shalt thou make it.

And behold, I, even I, do bring a flood of waters upon the earth, to destroy all flesh, wherein is the breath of life, from under heaven; and every thing that is in the earth shall die. But with thee will I establish my covenant; and thou shalt come into the ark, thou, and thy sons, and thy wife, and thy sons' wives with thee.

And of every living thing of all flesh, two of every sort shalt thou bring into the ark, to keep them alive with thee; they shall be male and female. Of fowls after their kind, and of cattle after their kind, of every creeping thing of the earth after his kind, two of every sort shall come unto thee, to keep them alive. And take thou unto thee of all food that is eaten, and thou shalt gather it to thee; and it shall be for food for thee, and for them.

Thus did Noah; according to all that God commanded him, so did he. And Noah was six hundred years old when the flood of waters was upon the earth.

In the six hundredth year of Noah's life, in the second month, the seventeenth day of the month, the same day were all the fountains of the great deep broken up, and the windows of heaven were opened.

In the selfsame day entered Noah, and Shem, and Ham, and Japheth, the sons of Noah, and Noah's wife, and the three wives of his sons with them, into the ark; they, and every beast after his kind, and all the cattle after their kind, and every creeping thing that creepeth upon the earth after his kind, and every fowl after his kind, every bird of every sort. And they went in unto Noah into the ark, two and two of all flesh, wherein is the breath of life. And they that went in, went in male and female of all flesh, as God had commanded him.

And the flood was upon the earth; and the waters prevailed and were increased greatly upon the earth; and the ark went upon the face of the waters. And the waters prevailed exceedingly upon the earth; and all the high hills, that were under the whole heaven, were covered. Fifteen cubits upward did the waters prevail; and the mountains were covered. And all flesh died that moved upon the earth, both of fowl, and of cattle, and of beast, and of every creeping thing that creepeth upon the earth, and every man.

And the waters prevailed upon the earth an hundred and fifty days.

And God remembered Noah, and every living thing, and all the cattle that was with him in the ark: and God made a wind to pass over the earth, and the waters assuaged; the fountains also of the deep and the windows of heaven were stopped, and after the end of the hundred and fifty days the waters were abated. And the ark rested in the seventh month, on the seventeenth day of the month, upon the mountains of Ararat. And the waters decreased continually until the tenth month: in the tenth month, on the first day of the month, were the tops of the mountains seen.

And it came to pass in the six hundredth and first year, in the first month, the first day of the month, the waters were dried up from off the earth; and in the second month, on the seven and twentieth day of the month, was the earth dried.

And God spake unto Noah, saying, Go forth of the ark, thou, and thy wife, and thy sons, and thy sons' wives with thee. Bring forth with thee every living thing that is with thee, of all flesh, both of fowl, and of cattle, and of every creeping thing that creepeth upon the earth; that they may breed abundantly in the earth, and be fruitful, and multiply upon the earth. And Noah went forth, and his sons, and his wife, and his sons' wives with him: every beast, every creeping thing, and every fowl, and whatsoever creepeth upon the earth, after their kinds, went forth out of the ark.

And God blessed Noah and his sons, and said unto them, Be fruitful, and multiply, and replenish the earth. And the fear of you and the dread of you shall be upon every beast of the earth, and upon every fowl of the air, upon all that moveth upon the earth, and upon all the fishes of the sea; into your hand are they delivered. Every moving thing that liveth shall be meat for you; even as the green herb have I given you all things. But flesh with the life thereof, which is the blood thereof, shall ye not eat.

And surely your blood of your lives will I require; at the hand of every beast will I require it, and at the hand of man; at the hand of every man's brother will I require the life of man. Whoso sheddeth man's blood, by man shall his blood be shed: for in the image of God made he man. And you, be ye fruitful, and multiply; bring forth abundantly in the earth, and multiply therein.

And God spake unto Noah, and to his sons with him, saying, And I, behold, I establish my covenant with you, and with your seed after you; and with every living creature that is with you, of the fowl, of the cattle, and of every beast of the earth with you; from all that go out of the ark, to every beast of the earth. And I will establish my covenant with you; neither shall all flesh be cut off any more by the waters of a flood; neither shall there any more be a flood to destroy the earth.

And God said, This is the token of the covenant which I make between men and you and every living creature that is with you, for perpetual generations: I do set my bow in the cloud, and it shall be for a token of a covenant between me and the earth. And it shall come to pass, when I bring a cloud over the earth, that the bow shall be seen in the cloud: And I will remember my covenant, which is between me and you and every living creature of all flesh; and the waters shall no more become a flood to destroy all flesh. And the bow shall be in the cloud; and I will look upon it, that I may remember the everlasting covenant between God and every living creature of all flesh that is upon the earth.

And God said unto Noah, This is the token of the covenant, which I have established between me and all flesh that is upon the earth.

And Noah lived after the flood three hundred and fifty years. And all the days of Noah were nine hundred and fifty years: and he died.

Now these are the generations of the sons of Noah, Shem, Ham, and Japheth: and unto them were sons born after the flood. The sons of Japheth; Gomer, and Magog, and Madai, and Javan, and Tubal, and Meshech, and Tiras. And the sons of Gomer; Ashkenaz, and Riphath, and Togarmah. And the sons of Javan; Elishah, and Tarshish, Kittim, and Dodanim. By these were the isles of the Gentiles divided in their lands; every one after his tongue, after their families, in their nations.

And the sons of Ham; Cush, and Mizraim, and Phut, and Canaan. And the sons of Cush; Seba, and Havilah, and Sabtah, and Raamah, and Sabtecha: and the sons of Raamah; Sheba and Dedan. These are the sons of Ham, after their families, after their tongues, in their countries, and in their nations.

The children of Shem; Elam, and Asshur, and Arphaxad, and Lud, and Aram. And the children of Aram; Uz, and Hul, and Gether, and Mash. These are the sons of Shem, after their families, after their tongues, in their lands, after their nations.

These are the families of the sons of Noah, after their generations, in their nations: and by these were the nations divided in the earth after the flood.

These are the generations of Shem: Shem was an hundred years old, and begat Arphaxad two years after the flood: and Shem lived after he begat Arphaxad five hundred years, and begat sons and daughters.

And Arphaxad lived five and thirty years, and begat Salah: and Arphaxad lived after he begat Salah four hundred and three years, and begat sons and daughters.

And Salah lived thirty years, and begat Eber: and Salah lived after he begat Eber four hundred and three years, and begat sons and daughters.

And Eber lived four and thirty years, and begat Peleg: and Eber lived after he begat Peleg four hundred and thirty years, and begat sons and daughters.

And Peleg lived thirty years, and begat Reu: and Peleg lived after he begat Reu two hundred and nine years, and begat sons and daughters.

And Reu lived two and thirty years, and begat Serug: and Reu lived after he begat Serug two hundred and seven years, and begat sons and daughters.

And Serug lived thirty years, and begat Nahor: and

Serug lived after he begat Nahor two hundred years, and begat sons and daughters.

And Nahor lived nine and twenty years, and begat Terah: and Nahor lived after he begat Terah an hundred and nineteen years, and begat sons and daughters.

And Terah lived seventy years, and begat Abram, Nahor and Haran.

Now these are the generations of Terah: Terah begat Abram, Nahor, and Haran; and Haran begat Lot.

And Terah took Abram his son, and Lot the son of Haran his son's son, and Sarai his daughter in law, his son Abram's wife; and they went forth with them from Ur of the Chaldees, to go into the land of Canaan; and they came unto Haran, and dwelt there. And the days of Terah were two hundred and five years: and Terah died in Haran.

This is the bare bones of a continuous and carefully chronological story from the Creation to Abram. To flesh it out the Biblical editors drew upon the J-document to include:

(1) An independent account of the creation

(2) The tale of Adam and Eve and the Serpent

(3) The tale of Cain and Abel, and of Cain's descendants

(4) Examples of wickedness before the Flood

(5) An independent account of the Flood

(6) The tale of Noah and Ham

(7) A short account of Nimrod

(8) The tale of the Tower of Babel

Index

NOTE: Items are numbered according to the notations and *not* according to the pages.

Ut-Napishtim, 203, 206, 208,
    247, 256

Valhalla, 269
Vegetarianism, 55, 125
Verses, Biblical, 3

Week, 62
Whales, 40, 41

William the Conqueror, 262
Wine, 274, 275
Woman, 92, 93, 99, 100, 102
Wooley, Charles Leonard, 203

Yahveh, 65
Yiddish, 293

Ziggurats, 367, 368